Prayer Bubbles

by Vickie Henry

Dedication

This book is dedicated to my husband, E.W. "Reb"
Henry, whom I adore. After 38 years together, I still
light up and feel a little flutter when I see him walk
into the room.

Once, when we were dancing in a quaint little resort
in Sardinia, Italy, I said, "If Heaven is any better than
this, I can't imagine." Reb said, "Oh, you have no
idea!" But he does…he has the sweetest, purest faith
of anyone I've ever known.

As I put Reb in God's Sacred Bubble every morning,
I thank God for him, my greatest earthly blessing.

> *"Wives, submit yourselves to your own husbands as
> you do to the Lord."* Ephesians 5:22

> *"Husbands, love your wives, just as Christ loved the
> church and gave himself up for her."* Ephesians 5:25

Table of Contents

Table of Contents

Table of Contents

Introduction

Beginning

A young lady once asked, "When do you know the right time to have a baby?" A wise, mature lady answered her, "When you know beyond a doubt that you are ready for your life to change and never be the same again."

"God, put Whitney and Wade in your Sacred Bubble! Protect them, take care of them, and help me be the best momma I can be."

Life is ever-changing. Events and experiences occur, never allowing us to remain in the same state for long. We are each a bundle of experiences, which converge to make us who we are today.

There is but one constant: GOD. God is the same yesterday, today, and tomorrow. And He promises to go before us in all things. His plan is perfect. God's Word speaks to each individual in a unique, special way.

My life changed dramatically the day I became a mom. In my humanness and eagerness to understand God's plan for me and my children, I began asking God daily to protect my babies (quite sure I'm not the only mother who does this...).

During my 30-plus years as a business owner, prayer was sometimes a challenge. Being down on my knees did not work well for me. My mind would race...a bold new marketing plan for my company, ways to bring in new business, ideas to brainstorm with my wonderful employees, and strategic plans with long-range ideas and goals would continually pop into my head. Soon, business thoughts took priority over any quiet ones. Listening to God definitely took a back seat to these great ideas.

One morning, as I apologized to God for robbing Him of our prayer time, that faint voice spoke: *"Write your prayers."* With the availability of many wonderful prayer journals, this was an amazing suggestion! My concentration improved dramatically.

Now, everyone prays differently. For me, visual aids have always been helpful, allowing me to focus not only on each person for whom I pray individually, but also to help me focus on my particular intentions for them. One day, while writing my prayers, I received another gift from God—my own special visual: a *BUBBLE*.

What a great idea! And it worked for me--not only words, but bubbles began to fill my journal pages.

Every morning I would pray, "LORD, put my children in Your Sacred Bubble. I know Satan cannot penetrate Your Bubble, LORD. Protect them and keep them safe. Keep them always close to You!" No matter what happened in our lives, the idea of that big bubble gave me peace. Oh, there's nothing like God's peace!

Have you ever noticed that what God begins as tiny ends up being huge? The pages of my prayer journals are now filled with at least 100 family members, friends, and mere acquaintances whom I pray for daily. I will not come downstairs in the morning if these individuals do not have the prayer covering God requires of me; each one is placed in God's Sacred Bubble before 7:00 a.m. It is my calling.

For years, this remained my special gift from God. I'd gladly talk about God's Bubble, but it did not usually come up in day-to-day conversations. God began to impress on me how powerful His Sacred Bubble could be to complete strangers - people in need of HIM.

In 2001, I bought one of the first Volkswagen Beetles when they began making them again. My 1969 Beetle had fallen apart decades prior, and I jumped at the chance to own another one, this time a turbo with leather seats, sun roof, and vanity plates ("BUBBLE"). I was so proud of it!

As CEO of my own company and an officer/board member of several professional and civic organizations, I had a busy schedule of meetings and events and would sometimes valet park my VW Beetle three or four times a day. Frequently, the valet attendants would comment, "Bubble, huh? So, what's that about?" I was always ready with an explanation: "Oh, that's the way I pray for people – it started when my children were babies. I would always pray that God would put them in His Sacred Bubble and take care of them!" I cannot begin to tell you how their demeanor would change. Many said, "I believe in prayer," or, "Good for you!" or, "Wow, does it work?" Of course, my answer was yes! Some asked me if I would pray for them or one of their family members. A few became very emotional; some even cried.

My prayer bubbles are so numerous now. My husband and I laughingly relate to Sarah and Abraham when it comes to the increase in our family. God has blessed us richly. Those two initial Bubbles that once protected, and still do protect, my daughter and son, now include seven beautiful grandchildren and a great-grandchild!

So, now I share this precious gift with you. God's Sacred Bubbles do not burst! They may get tossed about a bit and, occasionally, some of us may even try to get out of them. They remind us that not only does He hold us in the palm of His hand, we are totally engulfed in His love and His protection. So, relax and float away. And be sure to pray for everyone you know. Prayer covering varies from person to person, and can be felt strongly by those you are praying for.

God bless you,
  Vickie Henry
  Vickiehenry7@gmail.com
  www.vhenry.com
  www.GodsSacredBubble.com

Make Bubbles

On the recommendation of my speaker friend, Tim Durkin, I begin each journal entry with three things that I am especially thankful for. At first, *Faith, Love, Health,* and *Peace* were my first entries. You (and Tim) might think, "Vickie, that's four things!" but at the time, they were rote. In addition, I now note three things relevant to each day. Examples include sunshine, walking around the lakes with my dog, spending time with my twin granddaughters, pickleball, movie-date night, or lunch with a dear friend. When on a beach vacation, clear water, snorkeling, and swimming are frequent entries.

After writing what I'm most thankful for, *God's Bubbles* begin! Most are repeated daily, with a few changes or additions. The page is filled with scribbles, but I know God can read them. My husband, "Reb," is always there. Just below Reb's bubble is "Spring,"[1] which represents more than 3,000 babies in the U.S. who will be aborted that day[2]. I always pray for our Leaders and our Troops. "Baby David" began as a bubble for a severely disabled baby boy (featured in the local newspaper several years ago) whose caregivers had given their entire lives to his care, and grew to include all caregivers who are willing to give of themselves in such a sacrificial way. Other bubbles include Muslims, Egypt, Pakistan, the Philippines, and Christian ministries such as Groundwire, Strong Marriages, and the Achievement Center of Texas that God has called me to support through prayer.

Prayer time has become the most important few minutes in my day. Filling my journal is both a passion and a privilege.

I've learned so much from the people who are in my prayer bubbles every morning. Many of their stories bear a longer telling and are scattered throughout this book, but I would like to share a few examples.

* * *

Peggy – Enough!

Peggy recently had open-heart surgery. I placed her in a bubble every morning with the word, "Enough!" In addition to successful surgery, God has protected her from a drunk driver and other health issues. I beg God to put an end to her sufferings, though I must trust the words, "Not my will, LORD, but Yours…" Sometimes those are hard words to choke out.

My precious friend, Lisa, has been inside God's Bubble ever since she was
diagnosed with Stage 4 metastasized
breast cancer in her eighth month of pregnancy. The prognosis was grim. Research indicated
that persons with similar diagnoses lived less than 22
months. Lisa's bubble remains prominent today, right
next to her precious 10-year-old daughter Sofia's.

Lola, the mother of my dear friend, Linda,
reminded me of my own sweet mother--
just a really classy, happy, spunky, nice
person. While visiting Linda in Hot Springs
Village, Arkansas, Lola was rushed to the hospital for a
very complicated colon surgery; it was cancer. Immediately a new bubble entered my journal. Lola is still
dealing with treatment, so lots of prayer covering is
headed her way.

What can I say about my brother-in-law,
Hank, and my good friend, Gannon,
who I cherish and think of as
the younger brothers that I
never had? Bobby and Jo, Lynn
and Lynnda, Sherry, and
Jean Ann and Fred, all
cousins, mean so much to

16

us. I may not know their special needs, but God does, so in His Bubble they go. The same with my niece, Paula, her daughter Amanda, son Justin – we think of these families as our very own. And the list goes on!

Ultimately, I hope to inspire you to be creative with your prayer life. Converse with our LORD, and keep your prayer life fresh. Believe in of the power of prayer. I've seen the difference it has made in our lives. Prayer changes the **Pray-er.**

God may not always choose to answer our prayers in the way we want Him to. However He answers, we know that *His Plan is Perfect.* As my friend Donna says, "He may say 'no, go, or slow.'" God always answers in His time, although our timing and God's timing may be far, far apart. In the meantime, trust and obey...and Pray!

Lesson 1: Seize God's Blessings

"God's Sacred Bubble"
by Vickie Henry, 2002

There is a place of solace,
A safe haven of love -
It's called *God's Sacred Bubble*
And He sends it from above.
Unlike this world of hurting,
Of scurrying to and fro,
Of watching loved ones fade away,
And feeling Oh-So-Low,
God's Bubble is protection
From the evil of this life -
It shields us from destruction,
From worry and from strife.
So, when you feel downtrodden
And your pain is crushing down,
Run to God's Sacred Bubble
Where His peace and grace are found.
And, as you pray for others
Your son, your mom, your friend,
Ask God to protect them
In His Bubble free from sin.

Oh, Thank You LORD for comfort,
For your sovereign security,
For Your Bubble that surrounds me
As I travel to Eternity.

* * *

Mike is like Paul in the Bible reincarnated. There are differences to be sure, but Mike seemed to keep himself on the edge of prison life and, while in prison-- like Paul--he witnessed for God. He begins telling the other inmates what a wonderful Savior he loves with all his heart. My prayers for Mike are inspired by Ephesians 6:12:

"For our struggle is not against flesh and blood, but against the rulers, against the authorities, against the powers of this dark world and against the spiritual forces of evil in the heavenly realms." Ephesians 6:12

Mike has experienced Spiritual Warfare, battling for years against addictions and temptations. He has lived on the streets. Mike's bubble, along with his name, includes the words, "Ban Satan from him, LORD!"

"Therefore put on the full armor of God, so that when the day of evil comes, you may be able to stand your ground, and after you have done everything, to stand. Stand firm then, with the belt of truth buckled around

your waist, with the breastplate of righteousness in place, and with your feet fitted with the readiness that comes from the gospel of peace. In addition to all this, take up the shield of faith, with which you can extinguish all the flaming arrows of the evil one. Take the helmet of salvation and the sword of the Spirit, which is the word of God." Ephesians 6:13-17

One day, I was headed to a Fellowship of Professional Women Board meeting. Among the meeting materials in my car were copies of my poem, *God's Sacred Bubble*. Initially, I removed the copies from the rest, then felt God nudge me and say, "Take them."

I began to argue (have you ever done that?), "God, all of these women have seen this poem. They will think I am just blowing my own horn!" God said, "Take your poems to the board meeting." So, I did. During a break, I laid out copies of my poem for anyone who had not already seen them.

Mike's mother picked up one of the copies of my poem for him. At that time, Mike was in prison. Not a month later, she excitedly shared with me that Mike had circulated copies of my poem to dozens of fellow inmates. Several came to him and asked about this God who would protect them and told Mike they wanted to be in God's Sacred Bubble.

Wow, God! Once again, You took human weakness and resistance to obedience, and turned it around to accomplish Your purpose! I stand in awe and hope to pass Mike's fellow inmates on those Golden streets someday.

Today, Mike is out of prison and has a good job. He is a talented artist; he drew a beautiful picture of Jesus that is proudly displayed in my home.

> *"And we know that in all things God works for good to those who love Him, who have been called according to His purpose."* Romans 8:28

* * *

WOW

Janet Kinder was one of the founders of WOW, Word on Wheels, under the umbrella of Roaring Lambs Bible Study. At one Fellowship of Professional Women meeting, Janet shared information about her ministry, which visited retirement homes, assisted living facilities, and nursing homes, including Alzheimer's units. I realized that God had truly blessed this ministry, which began from grassroots and had spread to 17 different locations, more than 30 volunteers, and reaching hundreds of residents, but my immediate reaction was that this was certainly not something for *me*. Oh no, God put no desire – nor expertise – in my heart to 1) teach and, 2) spend time with a bunch of old people…oh, no, not me!

One habit I had learned from Beth Moore's Bible studies is to *ACT* on whatever I've learned from each week's lesson. The question following each lesson is, "What are you going to do with the lesson you've just completed?" In other words, DO the first thing that comes to mind.

Usually, my first thought is to pray for a specific person. Possibly, it could be taking a meal to someone who had just come home from the hospital, or make a call to someone in need.

That day, my God-nudge said, "Call Janet Kinder."

"Uh-oh, God, You are not thinking of me teaching in a retirement home?"

Not five minutes later, my phone rang. My good friend, Sue, had called to say, "You need to call Ann. She recently moved to Meadowstone Retirement Village and is feeling down. She really needs friends right now."

My next call was to Ann. The conversation went like this:

Me: "Ann, how are you?"

Ann: "I'm lonely. I want company. What I really need is a Bible Study like we used to have at Sue's home, and there isn't one here at Meadowstone. If you would lead one, I'd help you."

Oh, boy! What happened to no desire, no expertise, and no calling to teach a bunch of old people?

Janet Kinder immediately agreed to provide guidance for lining up WOW at Meadowstone Retirement Village. The staff at Meadowstone were thrilled and assisted in getting the news circulated.

What a lesson and a blessing! For more than five years, every Thursday from 10:00–11:00am, a dozen of us *old ladies* met in the pool room, opened our Bibles, and fellowshipped. These women talked easily about current events. When we shared prayer requests, most of them praised the LORD for so many tremendous blessings. "Wow!" was the perfect word for the blessing that came from being obedient (finally) when God called on me to step up to the plate.

One of my favorite encounters happened as we discussed knowing our loved ones in Heaven. We tried envisioning Matthew, Mark, Luke, John, Peter, and Paul. I said, "Just think, they will be our brothers, just like our earthly siblings. We will pass them in Heaven, know them, and say, 'Hi brother!'" In a flash, Tinsy, a loveable 98-year old with posture that most models would envy, declared, "They will be our OLDER brothers!"

> *"Consequently, faith comes from hearing the message, and the message is heard through the word about Christ."* Romans 10:17

Lesson 2: Follow Directions

Imperfect

I once heard analogy which has resonated with me for years. During a Weigh Down class years ago, the teacher said that our relationship with God shares similar characteristics and behavior as the ones we have with our pets. Our dogs bark at the wrong people, jump inappropriately, and are messy and demanding.

I believe this could be true! We – God's creation in His own image – have made a mess of our lives. We associate with worldly people and worldly ways, putting God on the back burner as we seek pleasures and materialism and feed our own egos. King David is one of my favorite examples: he had Bathsheba's husband killed so he could have her for his own.

Our teacher went on to explain why our dogs are so special—they await our arrival at the front door, waiting with anticipation as we return from an hour, a day, or weeks of separation. Their beloved Master is home! They jump inappropriately, they sometimes "leak" on the entryway floor, and yet the look of love in their big brown eyes makes our hearts warm and fuzzy, and we know we are worshipped.

This is what God wants! He knows we are FAR from perfect. He knows we fall way short of the glory of God; we do not deserve His mercy. But He also knows when we love Him more than any pleasure or material thing this life has to offer. David danced naked (some interpretations differ on this subject) in the streets proclaiming his love for God. God called David "a man after His own heart." After receiving the Holy Spirit, the disciples who were not (previously) particularly outstanding characters, had the strength to die martyr's deaths.

We very well may be similar to our canine companions – more trouble to God than we are really worth, but He loves us and He has claimed us for His own. All He asks from us is our faith, our love, and our feeble attempt at being obedient to Him.

"In it he wrote, 'Put Uriah out in front where the fighting is fiercest. Then withdraw from him so he will be struck down and die.'" 2 Samuel 11:15

"When Uriah's wife heard that her husband was dead, she mourned for him. After the time of mourning was over, David had her brought to his house, and she be-

came his wife and bore him a son. But the thing David
had done displeased the LORD." 2 Samuel 11:26-27

"But now your kingdom will not endure; the LORD has
sought out a man after his own heart and appointed
him ruler of his people, because you have not kept the
LORD's command." 1 Samuel 13:14

"Wearing a linen ephod, David was dancing before the
LORD with all his might..." 2 Samuel 6:14

Any Space Can Be God's Space

Our downstairs bathroom is decorated in "doggy chic," which began when I spoke at a hardware industry conference in Indianapolis. While walking through the convention center, where many vendors displayed their products, I spied a toilet seat. It was so cute. The seat was hand painted black and white, with cute little doggies all over it. The conference coordinator saw me admiring the seat and, a couple of weeks later, it was delivered to my home. Thus began a redecorating project where our small bathroom was converted from a rather bland beige and pink with a few angels placed on shelves, to a black and white doggy room.

One of my friends said, "How do you think God feels about you replacing those angels with dogs?" My conscience did not tug at me at all. As with all rooms in our home, even this room is dedicated to God. There are cute little framed pictures of our doggie Emma. One sign shares dog wisdom as follows, "If you can't eat it or play with it, pee on it and walk away." On the counter is a Christian tract entitled *Will We See Our Pets in Heaven?* My hope is that someone will read this little pamphlet and God will speak to them through it. In summary, the message is that no one (except God!) knows for sure, but the important thing is to make absolutely sure we are going there. How sad to think Fido, Max, or Emma would be excitedly awaiting our arrival and we go to a different place…

> *"For God so loved the world that he gave his one and only Son, that whoever believes in him shall not perish but have eternal life. For God did not send his Son into the world to condemn the world, but to save the world through him."* John 3:16-17

> *"I give them eternal life, and they shall never perish; no one will snatch them out of my hand."* John 10:28

Lesson 3: "Don't Cry Over Anything that Can't Cry Back"

Lesson Three's title is a quote that my mother said often. With maturity, it has become one of my favorite quotes as well…now that my mother is not around me to remind me, I say it to myself.

Prayer bubbles are not exclusive to individual people. Our world is full of news and issues that challenge any Christian heart.

It's Just Stuff

Bette Midler has a silly little book, now out of print, called *The Divine Ms. M.* It is beautifully illustrated. She tells about a little red-headed infant who was born adorned with wearing high heels and from Day One of her life, this baby said only one word – MORE!

No one (else) in my Sacred Bubbles can take credit for this particular lesson. What does this tell me? Maybe this is a lesson near and dear to my heart, a lesson I have yet to learn. God's still working on me.

George Carlin was one of my favorite comedians, in his early years. My all-time favorite of Carlin's routines was about STUFF. He humorously said things such as, "Our house is a place for all of our stuff. Sometimes, we don't have room in our house for all of our stuff, so what do we do? We buy a bigger house! We may rent a storage unit for the stuff we don't have room for. Can you believe that people are making a living just by keeping an eye on your stuff? Traveling with your stuff is a problem. You decide to take only the stuff you will need on your vacation. Soon, two big bags are full, and you have stuffed your carry-on with stuff. Of course, your pockets are overflowing. What's the first thing you do when you get to your hotel room? You put away all your stuff! Sometimes we have lots of closets, cabinets, and shelves – more places than stuff. What do we do? We go out and buy more stuff to fill up those empty spaces!"

These are astute, albeit funny, observations; however, "You've never seen a U-Haul behind a hearse." We will leave the world just as we came in--with nothing. We cannot take it with us! God has all the provisions we will ever need waiting for us in Heaven.

"For we brought nothing into the world, and we can take nothing out of it." 1 Timothy 6:7

In the 1986 movie *Little Shop of Horrors³,* there is an extraterrestrial plant named Audrey II that was always hungry and had to be fed. In the beginning, Audrey II ate almost anything, plant food, then human food. It was never satisfied. Before long, Audrey II wanted people! Human beings were sacrificed to keep Audrey II happy. It grew larger and wanted more and more and more. You'll have to see the movie to find out the ending, but it has significant meaning in today's world. When I'm out and about doing errands and there is time to burn, shopping is one of the first things that comes to my mind. One day, when a friend called and asked what I was doing, I laughed and said, "I'm feeding Audrey II!"

Way too much focus is on materialism. We can downplay its strong grip all we want, but the fact is it's one of the most serious addictions in America today. Alcoholism and pornography, even gluttony, may be called "ugly" in today's society, but shopping and overspending – that's just *the way we are,* right? No, it's definitely NOT God's plan for us!

One of the very worst examples of our obsession with material things happened on Black Friday 2008, as an "out of control" mob of frenzied shoppers smashed through the front doors of the Long Island

Wal-Mart and trampled an employee. Several employees were knocked to the ground, while others climbed atop vending machines to avoid the crush. When the madness ended, 34-year-old Jdimytai Damour was dead and four shoppers, including an 8-months pregnant woman, were injured. The store manager was quoted saying, "He was bum-rushed by 200 people. They took the doors off the hinges. He (Jyimytai) was trampled and killed in front of me. They took me down too…I didn't know if I was going to live through it. I literally had to fight people off my back!"[4] In an attempt to slow the traffic, nervous employees formed a human chain inside the entrance. The mob quickly overwhelmed workers. Despite the tragedy, shoppers were upset that Wal-Mart closed their doors for a few hours to remove Mr. Damour's body.

This subject is well worthy of its own bubble prayer. Let's make a promise today to pray for each of us to focus on God, our Creator, and not on the things that have been created.

> *"Therefore I tell you, do not worry about your life, what you will eat or drink; or about your body, what you will wear. Is not life more than food, and the body more than clothes? Look at the birds of the air; they do not sow or reap or store away in barns, and yet your heav-*

enly Father feeds them. Are you not much more valua-
ble than they? Can any one of you by worrying add a
single hour to your life?

"And why do you worry about clothes? See how the
flowers of the field grow. They do not labor or spin. Yet
I tell you that not even Solomon in all his splendor was
dressed like one of these. If that is how God clothes the
grass of the field, which is here today and tomorrow is
thrown into the fire, will he not much more clothe
you—you of little faith? So do not worry, saying, 'What
shall we eat?' or 'What shall we drink?' or 'What shall
we wear?' For the pagans run after all these things,
and your heavenly Father knows that you need them.
But seek first his kingdom and his righteousness, and
all these things will be given to you as well. Therefore
do not worry about tomorrow, for tomorrow will worry
about itself. Each day has enough trouble of its own."
Matthew 6:25-34

Lesson 4: God's Plan Is Perfect

In place of the perfect life we envision for ourselves, we are living out a life that results from the choices we've made; yet, at the same time, we should acknowledge God's perfect plan for our time here on earth.

I adopted my daughter when I was 25. Life changed that day and it has never been the same.

* * *

Whitney

After eight years of marriage, people began asking my first husband and me, "When are you going to have a baby?" In the 1970's, very few couples opted not to have children. My prayer life was not as strong as it is now and I probably did not include God in this important decision. However, the words of Sarah to Abraham had great meaning for me. We grew tired of waiting on God to help us get pregnant, so we decided to take matters in our own hands—we decided to adopt.

"...so she said to Abram, "The LORD has kept me from having children. Go, sleep with my slave; perhaps I can build a family through her."

"Abram agreed to what Sarai said." Genesis 16:2

We turned to Hope Cottage in Dallas, TX. In 1970, abortion was illegal and adoption was fairly easy and inexpensive. We had asked for a girl; Hope Cottage even tried to match the baby's physical features to ours.

Whitney was born to a 16-year-old girl—her second pregnancy. Many popular books on the market say the mother's emotional condition has an effect on her fetus. They say to smile, sing, and read to your baby while in the womb, all of which have been proven to have a very positive effect on the fetus, the infant, and the child as she grows. I now wonder how negative is the effect of a mother who is immature, unhappy, and whose life has been totally disrupted by a pregnancy? Could that child be born feeling unwanted and un-loved?

We have spent a lifetime trying to convince Whitney that she is loved and valuable. She is probably the most unique person in my life. To say we do not share a common gene or thought process is an understatement. We are totally different personalities. If we were not mother and daughter, our paths may never have crossed.

As early as 18 months, this precocious child of mine could talk a blue streak and every time we saw a huge truck, she would say, "Someday, I'm going to drive one of those." And she did! The chills down my spine are indescribable when a jack-knifed 18-wheeler appears on the news.

Some years ago, Whitney attended a meeting where I was the speaker. Afterwards, she told me she didn't know how I could get up in front of hundreds of people and give a speech. One thing is for sure, if you put me in the tractor of a big truck, it would not move! There is no way those 14 gears would get me on the road. My Volkswagen Beetle (my "Bubble") was more my speed!

This Child is Mine
by Vickie Henry, 1996

This Child is Mine, God told me so
He sent her to me many years ago.

I had prayed for an angel, a little life sent my way.
What I really wanted was a doll with which to play...

Six pounds of pure-d'-spunk, topped with
a head full of curly locks
began waking me up in the middle of the night.
And soon, I found she walks and talks.

I've watched her struggle; I've watched her try;
I've watched her fall; I've watched her cry.

I used to catch her before she fell.
I used to be able to wipe her tears away.
I used to help her as she struggled.
But that was yesterday…

God definitely has a sense of humor. After becoming parents in our own timing, God gave us a "bonus." Four years later, Wade was born looking exactly like his grandfather, Vol, who passed away a few months before he knew his last name would be carried on.

As any adoptive mother will surely attest, the love we have for our children is a bond like no other. Carrying a child for 9 months does not make you love them any more than the 21-day-old, 6 lb baby that is entrusted to you to raise. My children are the joy of my life, especially now they have given me the most awesome grandchildren ever! Oh, yes – even teenage mischievousness has been totally erased by these children they have sired!

"Growing Pains"
by Digby Wolfe, for The Goldie Hawn TV Special,
1978

Here's to the kids who are different;

The kids who don't always get A's,

The kids who have ears

Twice the size of their peers',

or noses that go on for days.

Here's to the kids who are different,

The kids who are just out of step,

The kids they all tease,

who have cuts on their knees

and whose sneakers are constantly wet.

Here's to the kids who are different,

the kids with a mischievous streak,

For when they have grown,

As history has shown,

It's their difference that makes them unique.

* * *

Gay struggled to keep her marriage intact—after all, that's how she was raised; divorce was not an option—but it didn't last. In the end, she raised her son by herself. Being a single mom, Gay found herself growing in experience as little Chad grew into a challenging teen.

Our paths crossed when Gay and I joined the Tough Love program. We both needed help with our 16 year old boys. They were running with the wrong crowd.

Chad was arrested at age 17 and sentenced to 10 years in prison at age 18. Gay's only child would serve 5 years in prison, an indescribable heartache. Then, 5 years after Chad was released from prison, he was shot and killed at age 28.

Gay had just been to Arizona with her husband, Larry, another Tough Love advocate. The three of us met at the same meeting. It was fun to watch as they fell in love and married. We became friends and even did some travelling together. Gay and Larry's plane was late coming into DFW, and Chad called to make sure Gay was alright. They had two more conversations before going to bed, each call ending with the tender words, "I love you."

The next morning Gay's world was empty. She would never hear those words from Chad again. That was 14 years ago.

What worse call could any parent receive than to tell her that her son had been shot? Chad was at the emergency room. He died as Gay rushed to the hospital.

This was the first time in my life that I could actually feel a broken heart. No words. Nothing anyone could do.

The killer was brought to trial. Watching Gay sit through those grueling days of testimonies, evidence, and graphic descriptions was painful for all of us who came to support her. Following the guilty verdict, the killer yelled out profanity and insults at Gay and her family.

Gay was told she could write a letter that would be read to the killer. She did. Maybe it helped her, but she chose not to read it to him. Doing so would have meant going back to the Denton courthouse for another day. She did not want to do that.

As I circle her name each morning in my journal, I see a loving, caring person in that bubble. Gay is known for her awesome, spontaneous laugh. It was dimmed for a time, but when that laugh fills a room, it's very contagious. Gay refused to let anger and bitterness destroy her joy.

> *"Get rid of all bitterness, rage and anger, brawling and slander, along with every form of malice."*
> Ephesians 4:31

Gay has been an inspiration to so many of her friends; we've watched her relationship with God grow even stronger. She has accepted that there will be no grandchildren, no one for her to really call her own. In spite of this, she continues to look to the One who has always been there for her, our LORD and Savior.

We attended a number of Bible studies together. One particular lesson was on tithing—a subject where we all nod our heads and agree with Scripture, but when it comes to putting an envelope in the collection plate, our faith may grow weak. Gay left that study committed to give as she has never given before. She immediately set up an automatic withdrawal for her church for 10% of each paycheck so she wouldn't be tempted to spend the money. Soon afterward, she received unexpected money equaling, almost to the penny, the amount of her annual tithe! Even now, she continues to tithe faithfully and has been greatly blessed.

"Each of you should give what you have decided in your heart to give, not reluctantly or under compulsion, for God loves a cheerful giver." Corinthians 9:7

For Those Who Have Lost Children

Many people pass through our lives barely touching them and yet leaving a lasting impression. So it was with Carol Anne, the daughter of close friends Martha and Mallory.

In her late 20's, Carol Anne was diagnosed with cancer—a brain tumor. We prayed and prayed, even anointed her with oil and prayed some more. For more than two years she rallied, played tennis, and loved life. Then, she went home to be with God. What a sad day to watch as parents lost the child they had raised and loved.

Weeks later, when Martha was cleaning out her daughter's personal items, she found a message that Carol Anne had written. This message is cherished by her parents and by many people who barely knew her during her brief lifetime.

Heaven is a place where you can be everywhere and nowhere all at the same time. It is a garden that is beautifully maintained, blooming with only your favorite flowers. And, if you desire to pick a flower for a vase, a new one grows back just like that… only brighter and better than the first. Heaven is a place where there are no mosquitoes. It's a place where you can be alone to think or be with your favorite people. Heaven is a place where Christ stops daily for your morning study of the Word and leaves you with a bright glowing feeling inside. Heaven is a place where the bunnies and deer frolic. And there is no pollution. Heaven is a stroll on the beach with waves cascading up on your bare feet. Heaven is a warm fire and a cozy quilt with a cup of hot chocolate. Heaven is anywhere you want it to be. Just open your heart and open your mind. You will see that Heaven is right in your soul where it was always meant to be.

Much love, Carol Anne

* * *

Since my husband's daughter, Beverly, passed away a few years ago and we have experienced this grief personally, the reality of the depth of grief that comes from losing a child is much more real to us. Birthdays come and go. Visions of her first steps, first words, and the cute little nuances that were specific to this child tug away at her father's heart. Holding that baby for the first time, then watching her grow, with never a thought of ever seeing her in a casket in the front of a church. Parents are supposed to die before their children. Oh, LORD, is there a Sacred Bubble big enough to heal the heart of a grieving daddy? I place Reb in that bubble every morning praying that God will give him just a little more comfort and peace each day.

Lesson 5: God's Business vs. Busy-ness

Everything God teaches, everything He stands for, and how He wants us to live our lives is opposite of what the world teaches, what the world applauds, and how the world says we should live our lives. Billboards tell us to go for the gusto, life is short, and just do it. Just do what? What we want. God tells us to love Him with all our heart and soul and mind and to love others as ourselves. He tells us to worry about nothing, but to come to Him with our prayers night and day and He will give us comfort and peace.

Being resistant to God is something I have struggled with more than once, but each time the struggling has yielded a great lesson.

> *"We hear that some among you are idle and disruptive. They are not busy; they are busybodies."* 2 Thessalonians 3:11

> *"'Teach me, and I will be quiet; show me where I have been wrong.'"* Job 6:24

Begin Each Day With Prayer

Being the CEO of Feedback Plus, the company I owned for over 30 years, was an honor. During meetings with other CEO's, I would hear complaints and grumblings regarding their "awful employees" and the challenges of managing people. At those times, I would whisper a silent prayer and thank God for sending the most wonderful people to our company.

However, business ownership also included constraints on my personal time. I became a slave to my planner. Not to be put off, God tugged at me to begin every business day with prayer. ("But God…that would mean a commitment to be at the office at a specific time every single day!")

Soon, a compromise came to mind. Monday morning was always reserved for our executive meeting, and the five others involved had no issue with beginning our meeting with prayer. Easy enough! God should be fine with that!

A few weeks passed with God's continual nudging to pray every morning. Following the prayer at one Monday meeting, Joanie said, "I love this! I wish we could do it every morning." I choked out, "Great idea. Let's do it." That was over 20 years ago. Even now, as retirees with fun travel schedules, Joanie and I still pray together *most* mornings. We've been known to pray through the internet or long-distance, whether sitting on an upside down sailboat in Grand Cayman or on top of Pike's Peak.

The lesson is this: the very calling that we resist often becomes our greatest blessing. We thank God that we can pray to Him anytime anywhere.

* * *

Joanie is in God's Sacred Bubble every morning in my journal. Prayer covering had been especially important during the decade where she cared for her husband of 50 years as he suffered through tremendous health problems. Steve is now pain free in Eternity with our Father.

Joanie

"A Little Joanie in our Lives"
by Vickie Henry

Hat's off to Joanie!
Our confidante and friend...

Our rock in the midst of chaos,
Whose compassion has no end.

Respect and love and honor –
All things we have for you…
We go to you if the copier is broken
And we go to you for our paychecks too!

How do we say "thank you"
For the many things you do -
For all the smiles and all the trials
That you have seen us through.

God knows how we appreciate
That throughout our joys and strife
He has been so good and generous
To put a little Joanie in our life!

"Call to me and I will answer you and tell you great and unsearchable things you do not know." Jeremiah 33:3

"Observe the commands of the LORD your God, walking in obedience to him and revering him." Deuteronomy 8:6

"Give thanks to the LORD, for he is good; his love endures forever." 1 Chronicles 16:34

* * *

Some of the people in the Sacred Bubbles for whom I pray every morning are my closest and dearest friends and family members. Others are encounters as my day unfolds. Our lives are like a Spider Web — some people touch us and set our entire world to trembling. We are never truly the same again.

Trish

I met Trish in a little boutique in Hot Springs Village, Arkansas. She was filling in for her daughter, who owned the shop.

Trish was sad. She shared with me that her husband had just had a stroke and was now blind. At one point, her phone rang, and she began to tremble, on the verge of tears. She told the caller, "I'm so sorry. I'm so sorry. I don't know how I can help you." When the conversation ended, she began to cry.

Regaining her composure, Trish told me that her husband had a construction business, which included remodeling and various repair jobs. He had many customers and was very well respected. At the time of the stroke, several jobs were underway. Suddenly, in addition to becoming her husband's caregiver, Trish had to deal with customers (some who were impatient, exasperated, and angry) who wanted to know when the work would be finished. She knew very little about the business, including outstanding invoices, and had to bear the brunt of customers' frustration.

My heart broke for her, and she has been in a prayer bubble for months. I don't even know her last name. And I've never seen her again.

"'And when you pray, do not be like the hypocrites, for they love to pray standing in the synagogues and on the street corners to be seen by others. Truly I tell you, they have received their reward in full.'" Matthew 6:5

"For he will deliver the needy who cry out, the afflicted who have no one to help." Psalm 72:12

Lesson 6: Just as You Are

A parent's wisdom is never really appreciated until you are an adult (especially when you are a parent yourself). My mother used to quote this little poem; she told me she memorized it in fourth grade. She always taught us that each of us had a special calling from God.

Discontent[6]
by Sarah Orne Jewett

Down in a field, one day in June,
The flowers all bloomed together,
Save one, who tried to hide herself,
And drooped, that pleasant weather.

A robin who had soared too high,
And felt a little lazy,
Was resting near a buttercup
Who wished she were a daisy.

For daisies grow so trig and tall;
She always had a passion
For wearing frills about her neck
In just the daisies' fashion.

And buttercups must always be
The same old tiresome color,

While daisies dress in gold and white,
Although their gold is duller.

"Dear robin," said this sad young flower,
"Perhaps you'd not mind trying
To find a nice white frill for me,
Some day, when you are flying?"

"You silly thing!" the robin said;
"I think you must be crazy!
I'd rather be my honest self
Than any made-up daisy.

"You're nicer in your own bright gown,
The little children love you;
Be the best buttercup you can,
And think no flower above you.

"Though swallows leave me out of sight,
We'd better keep our places;
Perhaps the world would all go wrong
With one too many daisies.

"Look bravely up into the sky,
And be content with knowing
That God wished for a buttercup
Just here, where you are growing."

* * *

At Fellowship of Professional Women, we have enjoyed wonderful speakers over the years. Sheila Walsh was certainly no exception. One of Sheila's stories touched me, and the message continues to make an impression.

Sheila

At a speaking engagement, Sheila was preparing to go before her audience when her small son came toward her, covered with icing from the cake he had been eating. Sheila knew what it would do to her new beige suit, but she also wanted that last-minute hug from her son. Most importantly, she wanted her son to clearly understand that he did not have to be spotless or all cleaned up to come to her.

The message was clear: we don't have to wait until we clean ourselves up to run to our Heavenly Father. He wants us just the way we are. His arms are always open to receive our hugs.

Just as I AM, Without One Plea (excerpted)
By Charlotte Elliott
Just as I am, without one plea,
But that Thy blood was shed for me,
And that Thou bidst me come to Thee,
O Lamb of God, I come, I come.

Just as I am, though toss'd about
With many a conflict, many a doubt,
Fightings and fears within, without,
O Lamb of God, I come, I come.

*"But if we walk in the light, as he is in the light, we
have fellowship with one another, and the blood of
Jesus, his Son, purifies us from all sin."* 1 John 1:7

* * *

Peggy Jo

Seventeen and running. If anyone ever needed God's Sacred Bubble, it was Peggy Jo.

Barely sober from the keg party the night before to celebrate high school graduation, Peggy Jo took off early the next morning in her 1968 powder-blue Mustang. She was headed to a state she'd never even visited. She did have a job, thanks to the help of one of her high school teachers. And she knew one person in the state of Colorado – Marilyn – who would be her roommate.

Did Peggy Jo hate Plains, Texas? Not really. She had loving parents, a brother she adored, and people knew her as a cute barrel racer and a member of the championship basketball team.

In fact, everyone in Plains knew her. Growing up in a small town, she had always been surrounded by relatives or townspeople who held no surprises for her – or her for them. You've probably heard of *the town so small it had only one stop light?* Plains didn't even have that. The one light simply blinked, little more than a suggestion of possible oncoming traffic than a need for a hard stop.

Peggy Jo was not mad, scared, or desperate. She just felt there was more to life than she'd find in this farming town!

Manitou Springs was only a few miles from Colorado Springs and had an affordable apartment. The grand old houses along the tree-shaded Kiowa Street had seen better days. Most had been converted into quadplexes. Peggy Jo loved the huge trees! Who would have dreamed Peggy Jo would live practically walking distance from Garden of the Gods and could see Pike's Peak from her front porch!

The close quarters didn't bother her, even though the bedroom (which had once been a dining room) sat between the living room and kitchen. It didn't even have a door! There was no closet, so clothes were hung from rope rods in each corner. When Peggy Jo's mother came to visit, she was appalled.

At age 18, Peggy Jo was independent, living nearly 500 miles from home, and learning lessons from her new life.

Lesson 1: Racial Discrimination

Only one black family lived in Plains—the Moores. Everyone loved them. Coincidentally, this was also the surname of Peggy Jo's maternal grandparents, who periodically received phone calls meant for the other Moore family. It was common to hear her grandfather on the telephone, saying, "No, you want the black Mo's. You have called the white Mo's." He and Mrs. Moore would laugh about the misdirected calls. She was a well-respected customer at his general store and she would tell him all about the call the next morning.

In contrast to the hometown friendliness, Peggy Jo and Marilyn's two black upstairs neighbors would lean out their second story window and yell, "Well, if it is-n't the little Southern belles coming home." Their humor seemed neither gentle nor respectful. Along with fear, confusion filled Peggy Jo's mind. Why would any-one treat us like this? Even though it was what some would call racism in reverse, it was a lesson learned—

her first experience with judgment being passed based on the color – or lack of color – of one's skin.

Lesson 2: Sexual Discrimination.
Just like Saul on the road to Damascus, it was time for a name change when Paul became a *new person.* Peggy Jo was all grown up with a brand new persona. Henceforth, she went by "PJ." And she was about to experience the proverbial glass ceiling.

The job was okay. As a proof operator at a family-owned bank, PJ worked in a windowless office doing data entry all day long. Though she found data entry mind-numbingly boring, Peggy Jo never dreaded going to work. Life was good and exciting. A gal named Sherry worked next to her, so there was some camaraderie…until Sherry resigned. Then, the days grew longer and more boring. However, a raise came— rewarding PJ for taking on much of Sherry's load.

When a new employee was hired two months later, the raise was taken away! The bank president had thanked PJ for her hard work, then explained that he had male employees, most of them married, who needed the money more than a young single girl with no responsibilities. Right there, right then, PJ quit!

More jobs followed, as well as more glass ceilings to bump against, but there is still a part of Plains, TX in PJ. The stable, loving foundation she received growing up has served her well. This was God's plan for her and, she says, "I know He has been there every mile and through every mistake and every triumph."

> *"There is neither Jew nor Gentile, neither slave nor free, nor is there male and female, for you are all one in Christ Jesus."* Galatians 3:28

> *"I am the vine; you are the branches. If you remain in me and I in you, you will bear much fruit; apart from me you can do nothing."* John 15:5

Lesson 7: The Body of Christ

Small Group

Our Small Group Bible Study has met for more than 18 years. The group originally started when Fellowship of Professional Women announced that they wanted to begin Small Group Bible Studies throughout the Dallas area.

My hand went up immediately! We have a beautiful lake right out our back door and a dining room table that holds eight people comfortably—a perfect space to host a small group. Since the beginning, sometimes up to 12 of us have been crammed into that room!

Since my retirement is filled with travel and a second home in Hot Springs Village, AR., other members host when we are out of town. Carolyn's beautiful home and her southern cooking has brought new life to our group.

We meet every 2nd and 4th Friday. Our first study series was Henry Blackaby's *Experiencing God*, which was perfect for us—we bonded immediately. We've continued through Richard Wagner and Larry R. Helyer's *Book of Revelations for Dummies* (don't give a pop quiz!), Beth Moore's *A Hearth Like His*, and, most recently, *MARK,* the second of our Bible's Gospels.

Sometimes, during this special Friday time, I feel like Richard Pryor in the movie Silver Streak. Midway through the movie, amidst a huge fight scene, with dozens of people yelling at one another, firing guns, racing their cars, and running down the street in total chaos, Richard Pryor stands up, the bullets whizzing by him, and hollers, "Who is in charge here?" One day, I even prayed about this, "God, I have NO control over Small Group!" He answered, "That's right!" He was letting me know that He is in control.

Small Group has been – as members came and went – always under God's leadership. Our group has been in

God's Sacred Bubble for over 18 years, both collective-
ly and individually. Oh, the countless lessons we have
learned from one another!

We have experienced many of life's milestones and ob-
stacles together: a divorce, work issues, lawsuits, PMS,
pregnancies, deaths, marriages, illnesses (physical, spiritual, mental, emotional), and countless tragic and glo-
rious stories in the lives of our children and now,
grandchildren. We have shared joy, happiness, laughter,
tears, fears, and sorrow. We hold each other while we
cry.

When my mother died on a Thursday afternoon, I prepared for the journey to Iola, KS; however, I could not
leave until after Friday's Small Group! I desperately
needed these healing arms around me. I drew strength
from their love, soaked up their compassion, wisdom,
and peace to face one of the most difficult times in my
life.

> *"Love and faithfulness meet together; righteousness
> and peace kiss each other."* Psalm 85:10

> *"...not giving up meeting together, as some are in the
> habit of doing, but encouraging one another—and all
> the more as you see the Day approaching."* Hebrews
> 10:25

Lisa is our youngest member. In fact, when this cute, tall, slender 25-year-old walked into our group of ladies over 50, we immediately began to mother her. Lisa divorced shortly after she came to Small Group, then later remarried and wanted to have a child. When she became pregnant, we rejoiced with her.

The day we held her baby shower, she was diagnosed with stage-4 metastasized breast cancer. She was eight months pregnant. The statistics are that 1 in 8 women will get breast cancer. Who could have known it would have been our youngster?

Lisa and her precious miracle child, Sofia, have been in God's Sacred Bubble for more than 9 years. That's right, the child we feared might never be born just celebrated her 10th birthday. Sofia is amazing, with the wonderful faith of a child.

Lisa is a fighter. She still has regular chemotherapy. Once asked if she ever felt angry with God because she has cancer, her answer was, "Absolutely not! Why would I be angry with God? I asked Him to do whatever He could to make sure I would be able to stay home with my baby after she was born. I just should have been more specific!"

"The LORD sustains them on their sickbed and restores them from their bed of illness." Psalm 41:3

One of my Small Group Bible Study members, Lana, shared this prayer:

LORD, take me where YOU want me to go;

Let me meet who YOU want me to meet;

Tell me what YOU want me to say, and

Keep me out of YOUR way.

A Tale of Two Churches

When we married, Reb (a "cradle Catholic") and I attended two churches: Fellowship Church, though non-denominational, was very much like my Baptist upbringing, and All Saints Catholic Church. The Sunday routine was an all-day affair, dragging two small children.

After praying all my life for a husband who would be a Spiritual leader, God had given me one. I would follow this guy who is a strong believer, a fabulous step-father to our children, and faithful in every way. AND, women's liberation being alive and well at our home, he followed me to my church of choice.

The Sunday routine seemed to work for the first few years, but the day was exhausting. I finally called "uncle." Begrudgingly, I might add. Reb was never going to be an upstanding member of the local Baptist Church, so I went to Catechism classes. My teacher was a priest who was raised Baptist (we often joked about the differences and how we really loved it *ALL*). Instead of giving up any of the deep beliefs of my childhood, there was the addition of the Catholic beliefs and rituals… which didn't take completely in the beginning.

Reb and I agreed that our daughter, Whitney, and I would attend Roaring Lambs Bible Study, which took place at Bent Tree Country Club (in the bar!). The study is hosted by Garry Kinder, a well-respected businessman and a gifted Bible study leader. His ministry is now in its fourth decade. How God has blessed it!

Our first visit to Roaring Lambs Bible Study was memorable. Whitney was 16 years old at the time and had just shaved her head. More precisely, she had shaved one side of her head, with her first initial "W" monogrammed into the shaved side. Reactions were a quick glance at the teenager, followed by a lingering "bless-your-heart" look at me. Without hesitation, Donna came to greet us and said, "Would you like to sit at the table with me and Anton?" Oh, how I will always love her for that!

Whitney and I attended Roaring Lambs Bible Study for a few years and, after she moved from home, it continued to be a place of solace and refuge for me. I was being fed—Garry makes God's Word come to life.

Our Sunday routine became very comfortable. Reb went to Mass with his father, while I attended Roaring Lambs Bible Study. We met up afterwards at the University Club, worked out, and then went to Treemont Retirement Home to have lunch with his parents. We looked forward to Sundays, and it seemed to work well for us.

The Sunday following Reb's father's passing, I could not wait to get to the Roaring Lambs Bible study. After such a heartbreaking week, I needed that fellowship. Then came that realization—like being nudged by a sledgehammer—where God said, "Your place is beside your husband at Mass. His dad is gone, and I don't want him at Mass by himself!" What a good idea, God!

I sat by Reb that Sunday and I've been beside him every Sunday at Mass since. It has become a tremendous blessing. I love the Catholic Church. You see, this time my motive was pure, from "so-you-want-me-to-be-a-Catholic" to being obedient to God and open to the blessing His Church had for me.

* * *

Lana
Lana wears big hats. Her favorite color is red. She steps into a room like she owns it. She never sees a stranger. Lana makes everyone she comes into contact with feel like the most important person in the world, like they can do anything they aspire to do (and she will help them!).

When she was a newborn, she was nicknamed Susie--the name I knew her by. However, as author of a best-selling book on estate planning, she became known as Lana Sue. But for her distinctive personality, some might think she is two different people. A good way to describe Lana is, while many people see life in black and white, Lana sees it in bright, shining Technicolor.

Those of us who know Lana well know that, beneath those big hats, her big heart is still broken in two.

Lana's son Ty, her first-born and heart of her heart, looked just like a movie star. He was a gifted architect, whose magnificent award-winning buildings still attract attention from fans of architecture.

Ty's marriage was similar to the Samson and Delilah love disaster in the Old Testament. Their relationship had been toxic from the start. Ty was getting over a previous relationship when he met his wife, who was hardened by childhood baggage and no Christian foundation. He was ambitious, talented, witty, and on a fast track to success. As Ty achieved more success, the angrier and more resentful she became. During this time, their son was born.

Ty began going to work at 3:00 am and returning home at 3:30 pm to avoid Dallas traffic and to spend time with his son. He bought a red high-powered sports car, then later added a red high-performance motorbike! He told his momma, "I love the feeling of the wind through my body, such freedom!" At 4:00pm one Wednesday afternoon, an illegal immigrant pulled in front of Ty's motorbike. She got a ticket. Ty got death. Lana's son was dead!

Eighteen months passed before Lana could breathe normally again - eighteen months of a dark, dark prison called mourning. Friends gathered around. Her husband tried to console her. God was there, but Ty was not. She missed Ty. She wanted to see that gorgeous human being that she had once carried in her womb. She wanted to hold her son. To make things even worse, her grandson was withheld from her. This baby with Ty's blood running through his veins was no longer allowed to visit his grandmother. Such pain and misery and torment.

Even though the pain is still there, Lana sought counseling and created memory books for herself and Ty's loved ones. The ongoing project has been tremendously cleansing. The old saying is true: "After time, the pain lessens and memories take over."

Lana adopted several scriptures and made them her focus for the day, just trying to put one foot in front of the other. Some of her favorites are:

> *"I cry out to God Most High, to God, who vindicates me. He sends from heaven and saves me, rebuking those who hotly pursue me - God sends forth his love and his faithfulness."* Psalm 57:2-3

> *"Do not be yoked together with unbelievers. For what do righteousness and wickedness have in common? Or what fellowship can light have with darkness?"* 2 Corinthians 6:14

> *"So I turned my mind to understand, to investigate and to search out wisdom and the scheme of things*

and to understand the stupidity of wickedness and the
madness of folly." Ecclesiastes 7:25

Lana will always miss Ty. She will always regret not sharing her grandson's childhood, although now she has a wonderful relationship with him. She will always have a hole the size of Texas in her heart for the son she loved so dearly. And she looks forward to being reunited with him someday in Eternity.

The Faith of a Child

My son, Wade, was such a happy child. He was our surprise baby, the child we were told we would never conceive. After adopting Whitney, my pregnancy was a total shock. The Watergate scandal was making big news at the time, and people would say to me, "What do you think of that fact that Nixon has been impeached?" I replied, "Did you know that I'm pregnant?" Carrying the child we thought we would never have was one of the most thrilling times of my life!

When Wade was 2 years old, we were driving down Plano Road near our east Richardson home in our 1969 Volkswagen Beetle, with the trunk in the front and no air conditioning. It was a hot day, so we had the windows down. When we stopped at a red light, Wade saw the driver of the car next to us - a young man with very long hair. Wade hollered out in a loud, clear voice, "Hi, Jesus!" Fortunately, the light changed to green and both cars moved on.

I asked, "Why did you call that man Jesus, Wade?" To which my two-year-old replied, "Because he is! I saw him last week in the grocery store, too!"

* * *

Getting my little ones to go to sleep was a challenge. We would review our day, read stories, then say prayers. Then came "one more drink of water," another trip to the bathroom, "one more kiss, please," and "I'm not sleepy." Bedtime sometimes took a good hour. It was exhausting! One night, in a state of desperation, I decided to try something different, something including God – surely this would work! My prayer was, "Dear LORD, we know that Wade has so much trouble going to sleep. Tonight, the minute his head hits the pillow he will be sound asleep." Wade dramatically threw himself back on his pillow, lay still for 10 seconds, sat straight back up and said, "That didn't work. Try it again!"

* * *

My children were very young when I divorced and began dating my husband, Reb. A year had passed since Reb's wife died of cancer, and he had three older daughters of his own. He told me he never had problems getting his children to go to bed; they fell sound asleep following story time (he could tell some great stories…) I was baffled as to how his well-behaved daughters stayed in their beds once they were put in them. Until…he admitted that he lay down with them. Well, now, that would work! My children would have been perfectly content in their bed if I was willing to sleep with them.

* * *

When our first granddaughter, Barbra, was born, everything we were told about the blessings of having grandchildren came true. We fell in love with this little 5 ½ pound miracle immediately! Every move, every word she attempted to utter was so special.

One Christmas Eve, a month before her second birthday, we kept Barbra overnight. She was beginning to say a few words. Over and over again, we talked about *the Christmas story*. It was important that she understood there was more to Christmas than Santa Claus and presents. As her bedtime approached, we cuddled in the big rocking chair in my bedroom. Her eyes were getting heavy. One more time – I just had to do it – I asked, "Barbra, tell me whose birthday it is tomorrow." She looked at me, wanting to please, but searching her little innocent mind for the answer I wanted to hear. Finally, with great gusto, she said, "Chuck E. Jesus!" (she had just been to Chuck E. Cheese) to which I replied, "Perfect!" and gave her a big hug.

* * *

When Barbra and Amber were young, they stayed overnight with us fairly often since their home was a couple of hours away. They would stay with us for two whole weeks in the summer for the Country Place Sports Camp. We loved having them. They did not attend church regularly, so, as grandparents, we agreed to give them an extra dose of Christianity during the times they spent with us.

My good friend, Wanda, suggested to me that we say *The Believer's Prayer* with these little girls, just to make sure they were absolutely clear regarding the plan of salvation. That night, all three of us kneeling beside their bed, I began, "LORD Jesus, I want to know You personally. Thank You for dying on the cross for my sins. I open the door to my life to You and ask You to come in as my Savior and LORD. Take control of my life. Thank You for forgiving my sins and giving me eternal life. Make me the kind of person You want me to be." After the first sentence had left my mouth, Barbra said, "We've already done this, Grandma!"

* * *

One year, during Christmas time, we decorated gingerbread houses and we baked a large sheet cake. We cut the cake in half so both Barbra and Amber could decorate their own *Happy Birthday Cake*. The plan was to have a birthday party for Jesus following the girls' nap time. The cakes were beautiful, each very unique. Nap time went as planned and, when all three of us awoke, it was time for the party. Barbra and I dug into our cake. but little Amber didn't touch hers. She seemed appalled that we would eat so readily. Finally, she exclaimed, "You guys, I think if we wait a little bit longer, He might show up!"

* * *

Our grandson, Max, has incredible faith (see his contribution to this book in the Afterward). When he was five years old, Max and I had just arrived home from the grocery store with items for our family

Easter luncheon. Max pointed to the Easter Cross that we proudly displayed by the side of our driveway and asked, "What does that mean, *'CHRIST IS RISEN?'*" I explained that even though Jesus Christ had died for our sins, He arose and is now living in Heaven with His Father, God. Max looked at me with all the wonder of a child and he exclaimed, "I'm going to tell people about that!" To which I replied, "You do that!"

I proceeded to carry groceries inside. When I returned for the second load, Max was nowhere to be seen! Panic took hold of my soul! I scanned the neighborhood and simply couldn't believe my eyes! This little five-year-old was going door-to-door telling all of our neighbors that Christ is risen! Hallelujah!

* * *

A few years ago, as Max related the story of Jesus walking on the water, and how Peter wanted to walk on the water with Him. He said, very matter-of-factly, "If Peter hadn't taken his eyes off Jesus, he wouldn't have started to sink!"

* * *

Max's sister Stella was born when he was aged six, followed two years later by twin sisters, Hannah and Ava. They lived only six blocks from us, so my morning walk included spending time with my grandchildren.

One morning, there was the most beautiful sunrise. I saw Stella near the front door and hollered, "Stella, come quick, look at this beautiful sunrise!" That look of wonder on a child's face! Oh, there's nothing like it! Stella was awed and very curious. She said, "Did YOU do that?" I said, "No Stella, GOD did that!" She said, "I've never met Him!" She was only 2 years old. I said, "You will!"

* * *

My good friend, Vicky, took a trip to the Holy Lands some years back. When she returned, her 4-year-old niece, Matalee, asked, "Aunt Vicky, where did you go?"

Vicky explained that she had gone where Jesus had lived and walked on this earth. Matalee said, "Oh, did you see Jesus?" Vicky told her no, that Jesus had died on the cross for our sins and had risen from the dead and was in Heaven. To which this precious 4-year-old replied, "You should have gone sooner!"

* * *

When do we lose this innocence, this childlike faith? We must try to do everything in God's power to re-ignite this wonder of God's creation and goodness.

When my daughter, Whitney, was little, we were lying on the hood of our car looking up at the sky. Whitney said, "Momma, what's that?" Nothing special caught my eyes. She kept asking, saying, "Momma, it's so beautiful! Look at it! It's so round and it's so yellow!"

It was the moon.

I've seen the moon differently every night since because my daughter brought my attention to it years ago and thought it was such a special thing. I pray to see the wonders of God through childlike eyes.

> *"So in Christ Jesus you are all children of God through faith,"* Galatians 3:26

Lesson 8: Reflection of His Love

Poetry is very special to me. I love to read it and writing poetry is one of my favorite creative outlets. Of all the poems I've authored and all the poetry I've read, my very favorite was written by my beloved sister, Erma Josephine Nichols. And nothing says, "Reflection of His Love" any better.

"A Lifetime"
by Jody Nichols (Vickie's sister), 1990

It's taken me a lifetime, LORD
In striving for perfection

To find You only asked of me
A mirror for your reflection

That it was You, and not I, LORD
That has the task of changing

My thoughts, my moods, and hearts desires
Were Yours for the rearranging

So, I'll let go and let You, LORD
My mind in perfect peace

With the knowledge that my constant care
In You has found release.

* * *

I met artist Susan Conroy when she spoke at our church. She had worked as a volunteer with Mother Theresa in Calcutta.

Susan's artwork thrilled me, especially "Child in the Palm of God's Hand," Susan's sketch of our LORD's hands holding a precious infant. Mother Teresa herself wrote on each of the fingers of God's hands: "You did it to Me" to remind us of Jesus' words: "Whatsoever you do to the least of my brethren, that you do unto Me."

Susan Conroy's *Child in the Palm of God's Hand*, drawn in 1986 for Mother Teresa.

I purchased the print and, for years, I used notecards with the same drawing. In a way, it appears God had inspired Prayer Bubbles through Susan's artwork. His hands were like a protective "bubble" case!

No one could have lived up to my teenaged expectations for a husband. He would be Superman and Prince Charming all rolled into one person. After all, we grew up on fairy tales and Disney movies.

Everyone I knew was a Christian-- everyone except Bill. In my naiveté, I felt that God's primary purpose for me in this life was to bring Bill to a personal relationship with our LORD Jesus Christ. It was MY JOB. At the time, it probably added to our attraction for one another. I had a mission and he was fascinated – though later turned off – by my religious fervor.

Even before God's Sacred Bubble appeared in my prayer journal, Bill's name was there. The prayers lasted through 14 years of marriage. Although the marriage ended, my evangelical mission did not. Each morning I continued to pray fervently for his salvation, that he would *see the Light*.

A few years ago, as I created Bill's prayer bubble on my journal page, a tiny spasm of rebellion tingled through me, and I whispered, "God, I'm tired of praying for Bill." That was it. After a quick prayer for him and the others on my list, I went about my day.

That afternoon Bill called me. We talked often about our children and grandchildren, but he sounded different this time. He said, "Guess what I've been doing lately? I found a really nice little church right around the corner from where I live and I've gone for several Sundays now. I even bought a Bible! I've made it all the way through Matthew, Mark, and Luke. Now I've started on John. Sometimes, I have to read it over and over to make sense, but you know, it is really interesting." (Wow!)

The next morning over breakfast, Avis, my good friend for many years heard this story exactly as stated above. I said, "Just think, Avis, I was ready to stop praying for him!" Avis looked at me with such wisdom and said, "Think about this, Vickie…Maybe you just finally gave him over to God. Maybe you finally realized it was His job to save him, not yours!"

"So do not be ashamed of the testimony about our LORD…" 2 Timothy 1:8a

"Our God is a God who saves; from the Sovereign LORD comes escape from death." Psalm 68:20

* * *

Willie Nelson's song, *On the Road Again,* could be life's theme song for our good friends, Leonard and Liz. They put over 40,000 miles on their Gold Wing Honda motorcycle last year! They rode from Dallas, Texas to Alaska and, just recently, completed a trip around the perimeter of the United States.

Leonard

The world of motorcycling is very foreign to me, so I find bikes and the accessories that go along with them fascinating. Leonard and Liz's helmets are equipped with electronics that enable them to talk back and forth to each other. They listen to audio books and music. Their navigation system probably equals that of airplane pilots.

Leonard was the vice president of operations for our company for over 20 years. He was a super leader, and we knew we could depend on him 100%. An SMU graduate and member of Mensa, Leonard is very smart and talented. Everything he does, he does well. And what he doesn't do well, such as keeping up with his keys, his wallet, and his ball caps, Liz does for him. They are an excellent match!

Leonard's son, Luke, is a doctor. One day, he paled while looking at his dad's X-rays. All indications were that Leonard had pancreatic cancer. Three different doctors concurred on the diagnosis. Leonard had been feeling horrible, doubled up with stomach pains. All agreed that his gall bladder should be removed.
Of course, Leonard was in *God's Sacred Bubble*. He had been for years – we depended on him tremendously as such an important part of our company. At this point, Leonard's bubble had grown bigger and bigger. We

begged God to heal him, to give wisdom to all of his doctors, and to work a miracle in Leonard's body.

With the gall bladder gone, Leonard felt pretty darned good again. The travel schedule had been interrupted long enough!.

The follow-up doctor visits yielded some doubts regarding the "pancreatic cancer" diagnosis, and further tests were warranted. Ultimately, the doctors determined Leonard did NOT have pancreatic cancer, but non-Hodgkins lymphoma. Currently, he has no symptoms and does not need require any treatments. Yea, God!

So, Leonard and Liz are back *On the Road Again…*

> *"Can any one of you by worrying add a single hour to your life?"* Matthew 6:27

> *"Therefore do not worry about tomorrow, for tomorrow will worry about itself. Each day has enough trouble of its own."* Matthew 6:34

Lesson 9: God's Timing

*"God, put Whitney
and Wade in your
Sacred Bubble! Protect
them, take care of them,
and help me be the best
momma I can be."*

Every morning this was my prayer. It still is. No matter
how old your children are, they are still your children.
In fact, when they are acting their very worst (am I the
only mother who had terrible teenagers?), we mothers
tend to picture this child who is acting terrible as a
baby. We see the infant we held when they cried in the
middle of the night. I'm convinced this is God's way
of keeping us from smothering teens in their sleep
(just kidding…).

Children Growing Up

Mothers usually get emotional about their children growing up and leaving home.

When she is three, it's unimaginable. At age four, you can look at her and cry just thinking about it. When he's five and you are watching him hit that baseball off of the little tee, you want to hold on to him forever. At six, you send her off to first grade and tremble all the way home. At seven, you watch him in the school play and puff up with pride. When she's eight and she rides her bike around the block all by herself, you hold your breath until she gets back home. At nine, he falls from the neighbor's tree, and you hurt more than he does. At ten, she thinks she's in love with her 5th grade teacher. At eleven, he's excited about *Middle School* next year. When she turns twelve, she's sure she is in love with her 6th grade teacher. At thirteen, he's in trouble for jumping off the neighbor's roof into their swimming pool. By fourteen, you are beginning to see a side of her you've never seen before. At fifteen, there's behavior from him that you hoped you'd never see. By the age of sixteen and seventeen, that "empty nest" is looking pretty rosy. You begin to look forward to seeing what used to be that sweet little three-year-old go off to college and, at some point, get off your payroll.

In what seems like that breath that David talks about in Psalms, these babies that you loved and nurtured are adults. And you are so very proud of them. They have grown up to be wonderful individuals who work and love and smile at you when you walk into their home. Where did the years go?

Then comes the icing on the cake: Grandchildren! God's greatest blessings!

> *"People are like a breath; their days like a fleeting shadow."* Psalm 144:4

Career

Maybe it's not the best analogy, but retiring affected me emotionally, much like when my children grew up and left home.

Working was fun for me; there wasn't a job I did not like. My sales career began at age 7 as a door-to-door greeting card salesperson. I moved on to running my own firecracker stand, then later representing my dad's packing house business by traveling to small grocery stores around Kansas to hand out samples of cheese and, sometimes, hot dogs. Following a car-hop job, you could find me behind the counter at the local drug store.

Age 18 marked the beginning of my banking career. A newlywed and far from home, I was a banker at Citizens State Bank in Roy, NM, then later in Portales, NM. I became a new-accounts representative at Clovis National Bank, and eventually vice president of marketing for First City Bancorporation in Dallas, TX.

Owning my own company was not a primary goal, but when it happened, the elation was over the top. Buying and building Feedback Plus was an adrenalin rush like never before.

Mystery shopping excited me; I believed in its value and it was easy for me to sell – especially to my banking friends. The industry was new and gained lots of media attention. We were featured in the *Wall Street Journal, Good Housekeeping,* Oprah's *O Magazine,* and others. People were intrigued by the fact they could make money by "shopping," while evaluating the customer service offered at our clients' businesses.

We worked with retailers, restaurants, and banks. Any company with customers needed <u>our</u> service to know how their customers were being treated. This *HIGH* lasted over 30 years – how many people can say they had a 30-year love affair with their job? My company, Feedback Plus, and everyone associated with it during my tenure—employees, clients, shoppers, and people in our industry association – were a tremendous blessing and I thank God every day for them.

The thought of selling my company gave me such mixed feelings. My husband had managed the company for 16+ years, then he retired. I enthusiastically jumped back in with a well-designed, three-year plan to position the company for sale. One year into this plan, a competitor approached me with a great desire to buy Feedback Plus, Inc. His compliments included his need for employees and he knew my employees were the best in the industry (music to my ears, because I agreed wholeheartedly.)

When the new owner took over, I thought I would continue serving on the association board, consult, and speak on behalf of the company; however, none of these plans materialized. The new owner had a different vision for the company and soon, it was "out with the old and in with the new."

Although it was the new owner's right to run the company his way, my feelings were hurt for quite a while. Suddenly, whenever someone asked me what I did for a living, I could not answer. For three decades, my self-image and my self-worth had been intertwined with my company. Who was Vickie Henry? (Quick, God, put me in Your Sacred Bubble! I need Your protection. I need Your loving arms around me.) I cried out to God like David did in Psalms.

> *"Have mercy on me, LORD, for I am faint; heal me, LORD, for my bones in agony."* Psalm 6:2

> *"I will give thanks to the LORD because of his righteousness; I will sing the praises of the name of the LORD Most High."* Psalm 7:17

My friend, Connie, recommended the book *One Thousand Gifts,* by Ann Voskamp. It was on my Kindle before I arrived home from her house. By the next morning, there were 640 "gifts" listed on my praise journal—praises to God for all the blessings in my life.

Who is Vickie Henry? Easy answer…I am a child of the Almighty God, a follower of His Son, my LORD and Savior, Jesus Christ. This is more exhilarating than any company, any job, or any material thing in this world.

"Heaven and earth will pass away, but my words will never pass away." Luke 21:33

"Remember the former things, those of long ago; I am God, and there is no other; I am God, and there is none like me." Isaiah 46:9

"No one can serve two masters. Either you will hate the one and love the other, or you will be devoted to the one and despise the other. You cannot serve both God and money." Matthew 6:24

"Before I formed you in the womb I knew you, before you were born I set you apart; I appointed you as a prophet to the nations." Jeremiah 1:5

A Part of Me is Gone

A part of me is gone. Gone where? Scattered to the winds, no more.

We went through a period that I refer to as our "Funeralizing" years. We lost 12 family members in 18 months. At one point, when our phone rang, my husband and I would look at each other and say, "You get it." "No, you get it."

"Funeralizing" began with Don, my sister Rita's husband of 44 years. He had been ill for a few years.

Rita is fairly independent and she was doing her best to face reality. She planned to be a well-adjusted, social, and happy widow. Then, when Don he took his last laborious breath, Rita crumbled. She had been married since she was 19 years old, had three wonderful children, ran a beauty shop out of her home, and she knew every person in our home town of Iola, Kansas.

Rita asked me to say a few words at Don's funeral. Without question, we made that 8-hour trip from Dallas to Iola once more.

My sister was a mess. Rita was usually so organized and in control, but the loss hit her hard. Her home was full of family and friends who loved her and wanted to support her in her time of need. She cried often. In between the weeping, she cooked and did some of her normal tasks. When the funeral home called to ask for clothes to dress Don, Rita's weeping escalated to wailing.

Young grandson Justin had never seen his grandma like this. Normally a handful, Justin scurried around to help in any way he could, showing tremendous compassion for his grandma. He pointed to a picture of his grandma and grandpa in Hawaii, and said,

"Grandma, I really think Grandpa would have wanted to be buried in this suit." Rita agreed, then told Justin to get it so they could take it to the funeral home.

That evening. we went to see Don's body the funeral home. At least half of the residents of Iola had graciously cooked and brought yummy dishes to Rita's home. As with most funerals, the gathering transformed into a big family reunion, where we shared stories and memories.

The next morning, as we prepared for the funeral, Don's brother, L.R., who had come all the way from California for the funeral, said, *"I CAN'T FIND MY SUIT!"* His was a custom-tailored suit crafted especially by his personal tailor in California. L.R. said he had hung it in the hall closet.

About that time, we heard Justin's small voice from the corner, saying, "I got the suit for Grandpa from that closet." My sister, who had barely stopped crying for three days, began to laugh. And laugh. And laugh. She could not stop.

Next came a whirlwind of activity as we all tried to get L.R. dressed for his brother's funeral. It was a Sunday. There was neither a tailor nor a men's clothing store in

Iola. However, Wal-Mart was open, where we found a decent pair of beige trousers. Calls to family and friends yielded a size 42 navy jacket. Afterward, we made our way to the church.

When it was my turn to speak, I stood at the pulpit and shared what a nice guy my brother-in-law was and how very much he loved my sister, his children, and certainly his grandchildren. The music was beautiful, the pastor preached a little – complete with an "alter call" for any one in attendance who might not know our LORD as their Savior (my Catholic husband had never heard of an alter call until he married into my Baptist family) .

The procession headed to the Iola Cemetery. Drivers pulled over and stopped along the route – something still customary outside larger cities, where fewer and fewer drivers show respect for a funeral procession.

The graveside service is always a sobering time, knowing that the body we knew and cherished would be placed in a six-foot hole in the ground, cold and damp. Thankfully, as believers, we allow our precious faith to remind us: *Don's soul is not in this box; "Tonight shall he be with Me in Paradise."*

Bruce, one of Don's beloved sons, stood next to his Uncle L.R. Finally, hoping to lighten the mood, Bruce said to L.R., "You look nice." With a knowing smile, L.R. said, "Thanks." Then Bruce added, "But not as nice as my dad!" We all had to admit that custom suit did brighten up that casket.

* * *

Two weeks later, we buried our mother. Rita had been her primary caretaker. She made all the decisions regarding mom's nursing homes. She sold her car. She sold her home. She was a tower of strength during Mother's final years. And she received the blessing to be by our mother's bedside as she peacefully slipped into Our Heavenly Father's arms…2 weeks following her own husband's death.

After praying and praying that God would let me be at my mother's bedside when she left this world, I was convinced that He would grant me this honor and privilege, but it was not in His plan. It was comforting to know that my sister, Rita, was with her. And God had given me time with her the month prior to her leaving – Don's funeral and the women's conference in my hometown.

The timing was good for me – if there's ever good timing to lose a beloved parent. About a month before Mother died, I had been honored to be the kick-off speaker at a Christian Women's event held at the Boy-less Art Center in Iola, KS. Can you picture a known speaker from Dallas, TX, going to her hometown to speak in front of more than 100 women from across the great state of Kansas? What a coup! I had planned to wear my cowboy hat, but Rita vetoed my idea. Both of my sisters were in the audience. Friends and parents of friends were there. Several of my high school class-mates were also in attendance. There was only one problem - the only speaking I'd ever done was on the subject of customer service. These people wanted me to speak about Jesus!

My sweet Momma had always said, "Every problem we ever have in life is caused by one of three things: Sugar, Alcohol, or Nerves!" The night before my speech, I had a panic attack. I was literally doubled up in pain. Well, NERVES gave me fits the evening be-fore the conference.

Walking is therapy for me. In the spirit of *Forrest Gump*, I made at least 10 trips around the town square of Iola, walking and praying, praying and walking, and eventually stopping in the corner café for a cup of coffee. Each booth in this café had a tiny dedication plaque, although I do not know their significance. The plaque on my booth simply had the name "Bragg." Immediately, my mind flew to one of my closest sisters-in-Christ named Judy Bragg, who had told me that very week that she would be praying for me before, during, and after this special speaking engagement. Once again, Satan was defeated! A peace came over me like no other, leaving absolutely no doubt this peace was from the only One who gives such calm.

Just before I took the stage, I talked and prayed with Nancy, the meeting planner. My last words before going on stage were, "If I begin talking about customer service, please remind me that my subject is JESUS!"

What followed was one of the best and most fun speaking engagements I've ever had. Stories of my childhood in Iola flowed from my heart. How blessed I was to have Christian parents…to be known as Clarence and Pearl Hixon's "baby"…to grow up singing *The Old Rugged Cross, When the Roll is Called Up Yonder,* and *Amazing Grace* at the Iola Baptist Temple where I was saved and baptized.

I shared the story about tagging along with my sister, Rita, and a cousin, both 10 years older than me. What a treat for a 7-year-old - hanging out with 17 year olds! When they experimented with smoking cigarettes, I gained blackmail material! Suddenly, I could go any-where with them and get nearly anything I wanted from them - otherwise I would, "tell momma that you smoke!" This was the same sister who had devoted her life to serving others, playing the piano and organ at the Baptist Church, even started a bell choir at her church, then helped other churches start bell choirs. She fixes hair for the little ladies in Iola nursing homes. A stalwart of the community – no one knew Rita used to smoke! Now they do!

The event continued with wonderful singers and speakers for the remainder of the day. During a break, I drove 10 miles to the nursing home to see my Mom-ma. I said, "Oh, Momma, I wish you could have been there." My mother, who had been unable to form a full sentence for months, replied, "Honey, don't you think for one minute that I was not there!" She smiled the old smile that was getting fainter each day. Her frail body was in a wheelchair, bolstered by a big cushion to keep her from falling out. Most of the time, she stared at us with eyes that seemed full of wisdom, but didn't quite know who we were. Part of me believes my mother heard me speak that day. After all, we serve the God of miracles. He raised Lazarus from the dead –

do you not think He would treat my mom to her daughter's testimony at her hometown?

* * *

My mother is now with Jesus, the One she loved all her life. She used to wake up at 4:00 a.m. and listen to the Bible on cassette tapes that her grandson, Kyle, gave her. She would follow along in her own Bible, the written Word, to make sure that the guy on the cassette did not change or add to the King James Version. By 7:00 a.m., she was on the phone with me saying, "Vickie Lea, do you remember when the Philistines were fighting the Galatians and Samson wanted vengeance?" Even though I'd been raised on every Word of the Bible and believe it literally, every single story, my memory for these stories was not nearly as good as my 83-year-old mother's. For a good five minutes, the truth would come out of my mouth, "Mom, it's not really clear to me." She was emphatic, "Yes, you do remember! We had that lesson on flannel graph! I taught you that when you were in 3rd grade!" Really… At the end of the five minutes of truthful denial, surrender came in the form of a lie (God, forgive me…) and my response was, "Oh, yes, Mom, I remember," because I knew she would keep on and keep on until she was satisfied that her lesson to me when I was 8 years old had found its important mark on my Spiritual learning. God gave her the responsibility, just like all the rest of us mothers, to train our children in the way they should go and they will not depart from it.

> *"Do not let your hearts be troubled. You believe in God; believe also in me. My Father's house has many rooms; if that were not so, would I have told you that I am going there to prepare a place for you? And if I go and prepare a place for you, I will come back and take you to be with me that you also may be where I am."* John 14: 1-3

> *"Start children off on the way they should go, and even when they are old they will not turn from it."* Proverbs 22:6

> *"Jesus answered him, 'Truly I tell you, today you will be with me in paradise.'"* Luke 23:43

* * *

Not long after losing my mom, both of my husband's parents died, Ed and Dores. Oh, how we loved them. They lived in Dallas, so we saw them often. We used to play *42* with them.

One night, we received a call saying Ed had a heart attack. We rushed to Medical City to hear that "it is very serious." Reb saw his dad as they began life-saving procedures, then we went to the small waiting room outside of the emergency unit. A doctor came soon after and asked Reb if they should continue resuscitation. The doctor then stepped out of the room for a minute while we talked it over.

Wow! We immediately held each other and began to pray. We prayed together, then we continued to pray separately.

My prayer was, "LORD, please don't make Reb make this decision. This is so heavy. Making a decision to keep pounding on Ed's chest…how can we give up hope? Yet, how can we ask them to keep this up? LORD, please take over. We can't do this. Please, LORD, give us clarity. Shower us with faith and trust like never before."

Soon after, the doctor came back into our little room to tell us that Ed was gone. God had answered my prayers. He had made this tough decision for my husband. Reb went back in to see his father for a few minutes.

Soon after, the impulse came over me: "I've got to get to Dores!" Her husband of nearly 60 years was dead and she didn't even know it. I felt a sense of urgency to rush down the street to Treemont Retirement Home, run to her side and make the big announcement. Father Gray, from All Saints Catholic Church, had joined us at the hospital. In his calm voice, said, "Why don't we let Dores get a good night's sleep? She's going to need her strength during the next few days." Oh, what wisdom…

The week that Ed died was one of the worst weeks ever. Reb loved his dad dearly and to watch him grieve was torturous.

The Rosary service and Funeral Mass were both well attended. Everyone loved Ed and Dores. They were fourth generation Dallas-ites and were well respected and connected in the community. Their other son, Hank, came in from northern Colorado.

Following the services, we hosted a large crowd at our place. We live in a townhouse on a cul-de-sac, with little room to park on our street, so we hired valet attendants. Bringing food was not as big a tradition with the Catholic community (covered dish dinners on Sunday were the norm in Iola, Kansas); consequently, some of our food was catered. Thank God for the Marino family! Bea walked in with a huge tray of all kinds of homemade goodies.

This funeralizing time period was a lot of work! The main difference between planning and orchestrating a funeral compared to a wedding is, instead of having several months to make arrangements, we had less than three days to plan Ed's funeral, then repeated the entire affair four short months later when Dores died.

Dores had been a model in her younger years. In fact, she found modeling jobs for my husband as well. Not many people know that 5-year-old Reb graced the pages of the Neiman Marcus catalog wearing nothing but a Superman outfit. As a child, he wondered why he couldn't keep the outfits that he wore while modeling.

Dores had COPD (Chronic Obstructive Pulmonary Disease), and Ed had taken precious care of her. We had no idea how much Ed had been doing for Dores. Over the next four months, there was hardly a night when she did not need help. We took turns going to Treemont in the middle of the night. We untangled her oxygen hose, administered medications, and tried to comfort her because she was in so much pain. Reb was an absolute saint.

* * *

The funeralizing (I've coined a new word) continued with the death of our 40-year-old second cousin by suicide; the passing of two uncles and three aunts; another cousin who died from an aneurysm; and finally, the loss of Reb's beloved grandmother, Mom-Mom. In total, 12 deaths in 18 months.

We are reminded daily that this is not Eternity. This is not our Eternal body.

"Jesus wept." John 11:35

"But those who suffer he delivers in their suffering; he speaks to them in their affliction." Job 36:15

"My comfort in my suffering is this: Your promise preserves my life." Psalms 119:50

* * *

Losing a beloved pet is heartbreaking. We made that fateful journey to the veterinarian to say goodbye to our sweet Emma, a Cocker-Cavalier mix. For 14 years, we were awakened with kisses, tail wagging, and a look of love and trust She let us know it was the beginning of a brand new day and time for breakfast. What joy we received from Emma. We thank God for each and every day with her.

Emma had a heart problem; like most King Charles Cavaliers, her little heart was not strong. She developed Syncope—fainting as a result of a drop in blood flow to the brain. It was so scary to see her fall to the ground and lie so still. At times, we thought she had died.

Toward the end, I prayed she would die naturally. We didn't want to make that trip to the vet. Euthanasia is certainly not something we believe in. God tells us that He knows the number of days He gives us on this earth, and after death, judgment, and then Eternal Life with Him. We struggled with making the decision to end a life.

Will our pets meet us at the Rainbow Bridge? The Bible doesn't make that clear. Some people have found verses that give them comfort and they believe that yes, indeed, each and every little cold nose and furry creature will be wiggling and happy to see their mommies and daddies.

Company Sale

I realized that with each painful loss or death that we face, a little part of us may die. We are never quite the same again. When the company that had been such a blessing to me suddenly belonged to someone else, life did seem different.

Years prior to the company sale, a set of potential buyers had generated some excitement toward selling. Such nice young men! The deal fell through when we lost our biggest account—a longtime customer who comprised 55% of our revenues.

Suddenly, major changes had to be made. We had great employees with lengthy tenure; seven had been with us over 15 years, four for over 20. We had to terminate at least four, which was gut-wrenching!

My husband, Reb, had led our company for 17 years while my speaking engagements kept me busy, allowing me plenty of free time and flexibility to pursue other interests – long lunches with friends, spending time with my dogs, walking, swimming, playing with the grandkids. With the potential sale on the horizon, he saw an opportunity to finally retire.

Retirement was not nearly as alluring to me as it was to Reb. I simply wasn't ready. When we thought the company would be sold, my desire to invest a portion of the money in some small business venture, for which Reb was supportive. As the year was drawing drew to a close without a sale, we had to make some tough decisions.

Early one morning during quiet prayer time, the LORD ignited a fire in my soul that Reb should retire and, if I wanted to invest in some type of business, then why not my own?

Then a really wonderful thing happened!

Experiencing God Day-By-Day by Henry T. and Richard Blackaby had been my favorite devotional. Year after year, the daily readings spoke to me, and there was plenty of room for me to write. On December 6, 2013, the words popped off the page! It seemed like forever before Reb woke up that morning. I could not wait to tell him my good news! Few times prior had God spoken to me so clearly!

My favorite definition of *MOTIVATION* is when the push of discomfort and the pull of hope are in balance. That morning, I was motivated! My *push* was the feeling of not being productive enough, of knowing that Reb wanted to quit working, and realizing that the company needed reorganization. My *pull* was that God assured me HE would take charge. I could not wait to be a vehicle in His hands! With one quick trip to the copy store, these words were blown up and framed in a 16 x 24" poster. Reb was 100% supportive.

The devotional's theme for December 6th was "Not By Might" and the Scripture was:

"So he said to me, 'This is the word of the LORD to Zerubbabel: 'Not by might nor by power, but by my Spirit,' says the LORD Almighty." Zechariah 4:6

The devotional message, paraphrased for my poster, reads as follows:

> *God's Word came to His people at a critical time. They were a despondent, disillusioned people who faced a daunting task. Their city was in ruins. Their magnificent temple had been destroyed. They had no resources to re-build their splendid city. Then came God's word! He promised that they would, indeed, rebuild their city. But, He told them, the rebuilding would not be accomplished by their own power and resources but by His Spirit. As long as they had God's Spirit, they had everything they*

needed. The success of your endeavors will not depend on the way you use your own resources but on how you obey the Spirit of God.

Terri, my decorator friend met me at the office that weekend, and we transformed my office from a masculine, golfing motif to a cozy one, with area rugs, family and doggy pictures, some colorful pillows, and a small monitor on the shelf which played a continuous video of a warm hearth fire. The new decor was crowned by the newly framed scriptures hanging over the desk. This would be the same cozy office where four of my favorite people in the world, ladies who had been exemplary employees for more than a decade, would be terminated. God gave me the strength to plow forward and keep focused on the job that had to be done.

On January 3rd, only eight of us attended our 2014 kick-off retreat. Motivational speaking is my passion, so I set the tone with the *Chariots of Fire* theme playing as everyone entered the room and a PowerPoint presentation designed to excite even the most disillusioned team. We all missed the four former members of our team, but we knew it was *Onward Christian Soldiers*. PJ, our top sales person of 20+ years, walked into that meeting to let us know we had landed a new account - Michael's! After just reading *The Circle Maker*, I had literally walked around the Michael's store on Montfort in Dallas, praying and praying that God would favor us with that account. Yea! Another sign from God!

Nine months of momentum kept us excited. Then we lost business again, each account due to extenuating circumstances. One was sold to a larger conglomerate and mystery shopping was to be combined with the parent company. One client closed their doors. Two others had severe budget cuts, and mystery shopping had to go. Four great accounts and significant revenue…gone.

The morning we learned we lost the fourth account, I also received a call from a local competitor who had been showing interest in Feedback in recent years. Having never met him and having no immediate interest in selling, I hadn't taken his inquiries very seriously. When he called that morning, I was really down. Jesus's words, "LORD, why have you forsaken me" were ringing through my own mind. My response to Tom (not his real name) was "Great timing, Tom! I'm ready to talk!"

Tom said he so admired this "giant of a company" that he would do whatever it took to buy the business. He wanted to rush the transaction so he could take over before our lease expired in a few months. His enthusiasm was contagious. Aside from the two fine young men who we nearly sold to, all other buyers had only expressed interest in numbers, all but ignoring the wonderful people on staff and the exemplary reputation we had enjoyed for 30+ years. Tom, however, wanted these employees. His business was growing and he was delivering nearly as many mystery shops per month as we were at that point, with a tiny crew. Tom was working around the clock, with his wife working almost as many hours for his company as she did at her own full-time job. His work ethic was impressive and, as I mentioned, he was very complimentary and enthusiastic about my company. It seemed as if God was orchestrating the entire sales process—which was a first for both parties concerned.

My 30-year-old adventure had come to an end. I no longer had a "title" or considered myself an "executive woman!" What a different feeling. I was no longer on the board of the Mystery Shopping Providers Association. The new owner had every right to run the company as he chose and I was no longer involved.

After my first meeting with the new owner, I placed him in *God's Sacred Bubble* and I have prayed for him every day since, and continue to do so.

For me, the sale was the end of an important season of my life. After all, this company was like a precious baby to me. For 30 years, my waking thoughts were of business concerns and a sense of urgency to bring in new business, followed by cash flow and making payroll. Enthusiasm was the fuel for my motivation.

My Small Group met shortly following the March 14th closing. That day's lesson focused on struggling to know the exact plans that God has in store for each of us. Ironically I had just written these words:

"Selling Feedback"
by Vickie Henry, 2002

I think I will
I think I won't
I know I want to
Oh…maybe I don't
It's gone on so long
This roller coaster ride!
One day I'm sure
The next day I can't decide

I'm excited
Then fear grabs my heart
I think everything's okay
Then it all falls apart

So it is, LORD
Life is in Your hands
Who am I to question
Your perfect plans?

Retirement is much more satisfying than I ever dreamed it could be. Writing is now my passion, along with pickleball, kayaking, playing with my dog, travelling, and spending time with my grandchildren.

"There is a time for everything, and a season for every activity under the heavens: Ecclesiasties 3:1

Lesson 10: God Defines Perfect

As a little girl, my idea of a perfect life included curly hair, a pony, and long eyelashes. Isn't childhood wonderful? Mine was, but I know many people are not as fortunate. Stories of neglect and abuse fill our newspapers. Bad things happen to good people. None of us knows why.

As we grow older, the dreaded telephone calls are more frequent. Most of us have experienced the death of a loved one. Breast cancer changes the lives of one in eight women. Special-needs children sometimes need round-the-clock caregiving. Watching people we love suffer is tough. Our own suffering and losses are miserable. None of these things were part of our childhood vision of a life of perfection.

While on vacation a few years ago, I experienced an overwhelming sense of truth. First, God did not promise us a rose garden. And second, where did we get the mistaken idea that we know the definition of PERFECT?

* * *

Blue skies in Puerto Vallarta and the yo-ga class just ended. Karen had given me a book that her daughter wrote, and it was a perfect time to lie down on a chaise lounge overlooking the ocean and begin read-ing.

Perfect timing! Tammy Amosson is a gifted speaker, writer, and the mother of Jac – the subject matter for her book, *Special Angel*. I'm fascinated with how Tam-my imagines that Jac speaks to God...

"God, please help my mom and dad today. Seizures are tor-menting my body and, as so many other days, we will make sev-eral emergency trips to the hospital."

Throughout Tammy's book, she refers to Jac, who is severely handicapped, as perfect. Jac is unable to talk, has difficulty walking, and is plagued with seizures dai-ly. Tammy explained that Jac is God's creation and he is living out God's plan for his life. So, how could he not be perfect?.

Wow! Humility has never been my best characteristic, so this really spoke to me. How arrogant we have be-come to think that we – God's clay – have the right to define perfect!

What do we ask the moment a new baby is born? Does he or she have 10 fingers? 10 toes? Is everything working perfectly?

My husband, Reb, says one of the hardest things he ever did was to walk into the hospital room following the birth of his second daughter to tell his wife, "Beverly has Down Syndrome."

Beverly, Reb's perfect daughter, passed away at the age of 44. We stared at her picture in the Dallas Morning News. Seeing your daughter's picture in the obituaries is surreal. We held each other. We cried. The hole in a father's heart is unbearable. Only Christ's love offers comfort.

Welcome to Holland

Parenthood can be challenging in the best of times, but many joys can be found in the unexpected. The following was sent to me and illustrates parenthood perfectly:

When you're going to have a baby, it's like planning a fabulous vacation trip to Italy. You buy a bunch of guide books and make your wonderful plans. The Coliseum...the Sistine Chapel...gondolas... You may learn some handy phrases in Italian. It's all very exciting.

After several months of eager anticipation, the day finally arrives. You pack your bags and off you go. Several hours later, the plane lands. The flight attendant comes in and says, "Welcome to Holland!"

"Holland?" you say. "What do you mean, Holland? I signed up for Italy. I'm supposed to be in Italy. All my life I've dreamed of going to Italy." But there's been a change in the flight plan. They've landed in Holland, and there you must stay.

The important thing is that they haven't taken you to a horrible, disgusting, filthy place full of pestilence, famine, and disease. It's just a different place. So, you must go out and buy new guidebooks. You must learn a whole new language. And you will meet a whole new group of people you would never have met.

It's just a different place. It's slower paced than Italy, less flashy than Italy. But after you've been there for a while and you catch your breath, you look around. You begin to notice that Holland has windmills. Holland has tulips. Holland even has Rembrandts.

But everyone you know is busy coming and going from Italy, and they're all bragging about what a wonderful time they had there. And for the rest of your life you will say, "Yes, that's where I was supposed to go. That's what I had planned." And the pain of that experience will never, ever, ever, go away.

The loss of that dream is a very significant loss. But if you spend your life mourning the fact that you didn't get to Italy, you may never be free to enjoy the very special, the very lovely things about Holland.

When Sarah Palin spoke for the Pregnancy Advocate Center in Dallas, her son Trigg was only 2 years old. With Down syndrome, it took great effort for Trigg to pull himself up. He learned to stand up in his crib and then began each morning by standing. He smiles at his new accomplishment and begins to clap. Sarah then asked her audience, "How many of you begin each and every day by applauding your new day?" The thought crossed my mind that many of us are too caught up in circumstances to smile, let alone applaud.

* * *

Finnigan is in God's Sacred Bubble every morning. For 10 days following his birth, there was no word. Then,

Finnigan

the most beautiful letter came to my son and daughter-in-law, Finnigan's parents' best friends. Here are just a few excerpts:

First of all, thanks again for everyone's words of encouragement, as we do our best to keep our heads above water. As described below, things have been going well the past few days, but as the hours pass here at bedside, with our baby healing from an all-too-eventful first week of life, our thoughts still drift to darker places with relative ease. The kindness of your emails, voicemails and texts are much-needed reminders to stay positive as we walk this road.

Regarding our baby boy, one surgery behind us, both his heart and GI doctors are pleased with his recovery thus far. The worst part right now is that Claire and I feel like we are leading double lives, dividing time between being here with Finnigan and home with Genevieve and Anson. We want nothing more than for the whole gang to be at home together, not having to make these choices about which of our children are to be neglected at any given time.

Finnigan has been diagnosed with Down syndrome.

Flower children that we are, Claire and I took a very 'natural' approach to the pregnancy and elected not to participate with any *pre-natal screens for these kinds of disorders, feeling that we wouldn't do anything different (i.e., terminate) if they did turn up positive.* Holding our baby boy in our arms now, we can say without hesitation that our hearts served us well with that logic. We would not give up this beautiful boy for anything.*

We have never placed much value on emphasizing what Genevieve and Anson cannot do; it will be no different with Finnigan. As with our first two, the challenge will be to simply raise the finest human being imaginable - the rules of the game are only different this time around.

Our focus for now remains on a safe recovery from surgery, so that our family might all be home together soon. A long and unfamiliar journey lies ahead. We invite you along with us.

Thank you all for the continued love and support, keep the prayers coming!

Love,
Ollie and Claire

I've heard statistics quoted that 90+% of women go through with abortions after learning that their unborn child has a birth defect like Down syndrome. It brightens my day each time I go to Facebook and see the most recent pictures that Claire posts of her beautiful family, her PERFECT family...

"Be perfect, therefore, as your heavenly Father is perfect." Matthew 5:48

"Jesus answered, 'If you want to be perfect, go, sell your possessions and give to the poor, and you will have treasure in heaven. Then come, follow me.'" Matthew 19:21

* * *

Spencer

A fellow Kindergartener had a disagreement with Spencer. She pushed him; he pushed back. He looked her in right in the face and said, "If you push me again, I'll draw blood out of you!"

Drawing blood had been a frequent occurrence during Spencer's first 5 years. Diagnosed with a brain tumor at 10 months, he was not expected to see his first birthday. His grandparents live two doors down from us. We can usually tell the results of Spencer's MRI's and scans by the look in his "BB's" eyes. BB is Spencer's affectionate term for Bill Benson, his grandpa.

Spencer has spent so much time at Cook's Children's Hospital that he knows exactly where to go. He heads straight to the very drawer that holds the Band-Aids and picks out the one with the action figure he wants on it. Needles and infusions have always been a way of life for Spencer. He knows every nurse by name and he talks to them about Jesus. During the worst of Spencer's treatments, he tries to comfort the nurses.

While undergoing radiation treatment, Spencer's little head had to be locked down and anchored to the table every day for six weeks. I know Christ was in that room, holding his mom and dad as they cried.

Spencer's mom says, "He had five series of chemo for his tumor at Cook's, radiation at MD Anderson, and then back to Cook's for his bone marrow transplant – That's a lot of hospital stays over the past decade!" And Spencer has come through flying colors.

The position of Spencer's tumor determines if he can see well or not. There have been periods when Spencer is legally blind. If there are several people in a room, Spencer will call out each by name and listen carefully to determine everyone's location.

Spencer calls me "Ms. Vickie," and we've never seen him when he wasn't in a good mood. We've seen him bald. We've seen him stumbling because he couldn't see where he was going. We've seen him laughing. But we've never seen Spencer grumble or cry. One day, he had a sandal on his left foot and a boot on his right. I said, "You're lookin' good, Spencer!" With a big smile, he answered, "Well, thank you, Ms. Vickie." This little boy has such a delightful personality.

Spencer was probably one of the first to be entered in God's Sacred Bubble. This young man, who the doctors did not think would live to be one year old, is now 14 and going strong.

Why do bad things happen to good people? That's the age-old question that sends some people running from God. Why would a good God allow someone, especially someone so innocent, to suffer so?

> "For we know that if the earthly tent we live in is destroyed, we have a building from God, an eternal house in heaven, not built by human hands. Meanwhile we groan, longing to be clothed instead with our heavenly dwelling, because when we are clothed, we will not be found naked. For while we are in this tent, we groan and are burdened, because we do not wish to be unclothed but to be clothed instead with our heavenly dwelling, so that what is mortal may be swallowed up by life. Now the one who has fashioned us for this very purpose is God, who has given us the Spirit as a deposit, guaranteeing what is to come." 2 Corinthians 5:1-5

Lesson 11: Hope in the Midst of Hopelessness

Cindy Brinker Simmons spoke to the Plano Christian Prayer Breakfast only a few days after her beloved husband, Bob, died. I'll always remember her voicemail giving us updates as Bob battled cancer (CaringBridge.com was not popular yet). She would always end the message saying, "Oh, Dear Ones, whether Bob stays or whether he goes, all things are in God's hands!" On that early morning, Cindy spoke about the hole in one's heart after losing a loved one. She said that no amount of medications, alcohol, sex, or material possessions can ever fill this hole. It can only be filled by the One who created that heart, our LORD and Savior, Jesus Christ.

Gannon and Hannah's Mom

Diane

When Diane walks into a room, eyes turn her direction. To say she is beautiful is an understatement. She seems to have no idea how pretty she is. You can actually *feel* inner beauty radiating from inside her. At one time, we would have given much credit to her gorgeous blonde hair that framed her face and bounced as she walked--it definitely catches the eye. Now, we know it's not her hair.

The night that her husband shaved every bit of her beautiful hair from her scalp, he had tears running down his face. As the golden locks fell to the floor, so did the last bit of pride, ego, and self-centeredness. In their place, during some of the worst moments of their lives, came a deep love as Diane and Tim had never known before.

After only one year of marriage and the promises of life-long dreams, they discovered that no amount of hair on the floor could ever dim that love. Suddenly, they were closer than they ever thought they could be. Diane always knew the LORD was with her. There was no doubt that this thing called cancer was a monster that she and Tim would fight together. She was not alone.

The nightmare began when Diane experienced painful symptoms which worsened as her attempts at getting pregnant became challenging. She asked for an ultrasound to find out what was wrong. Diagnosis: a mass and fluid in her uterus. Unsure of what was going on, doctors ordered more tests. A few possible causes were mentioned, cancer being least likely. After all, Diane was young and vibrant and had no family history of cancer. The next few weeks were a whirlwind of tests and a roller coaster of emotions. Diane felt like a robot going from doctor to doctor, lab to lab, then on to exploratory surgery. She said, "Sometimes, I had to remind myself to just breathe."

Prior to surgery, Diane reminded the doctor that having a family was very important to her and Tim. He said he understood, but made it clear that her well-being would be their primary objective; they would attempt to preserve fertility, but first and foremost would be to make decisions in her best interest.

Just before being wheeled into surgery, yet another doctor appeared on the scene. He introduced himself as her oncologist. "Oncologist?" Diane thought, and may have even uttered, "What are *YOU* doing here?"

Diane trusted God; she believed with all her heart that God was her Creator, her Savior, and He had always taken care of her. He had given her so many blessings: loving, Christian parents, a strong foundation. *But she was also human. She was scared!* She faced surgery having no idea what she would wake up to.

Diane woke up with one fewer ovary and fallopian tube. Next was another waiting period to find out the results of more tests to find out what on earth was going on in her body. She tried her best to stay away from Google. And she prayed.

Finally came the words that rocked their world, the words that no one is prepared to hear: Stage Two ovarian cancer. Numbness and shock surged through her body.

Prayer bubbles were being lifted up to God in mega doses. Diane's uncle, Gannon, is my best friend. He contacted me immediately, and I sent prayer requests to my Small Group Bible study, Fellowship of Professional Women, the Roaring Lambs Bible study, and every other prayer warrior in our circle of family and friends. Prayer covering was coming from all over Texas. Tim's family and friends were praying all over California and beyond. If we knew how widespread were the prayer requests for Diane, we would be overwhelmed. God's Sacred Bubbles were filled with love, concern, and begging, "Please LORD, heal this Godly young woman, Priscilla and Warren's daughter, Tim's wife, this Champion for You. Give her a peace that only You can give."

Diane felt these prayers. Along with peace that passes all understanding, a peace that only comes from our Creator, she had doctors and nurses and caregivers who treated her with dignity. They did their best to put her at ease.

Walking through the doors of the cancer clinic for the first time, Diane remembers thinking, "What am *I* doing *here?*" Quickly, these angels-on-earth came to her rescue.

Following her diagnosis, Diane and Tim requested to delay chemotherapy. However, a first round of chemotherapy was necessary, and then they would have to wait at least six months afterward to revisit their hopes of a pregnancy. They begged the doctors to give them one month for fertility treatments. One month to do their best to have a chance for a baby they wanted so badly. The reprieve was granted.

Three viable embryos were preserved. Diane says her favorite verse through treatment was *"And now these three remain: faith, hope and love. But the greatest of these is love."* 1 Corinthians 13:13

The three frozen embryos were nicknamed Faith, Hope & Love.

After months of chemotherapy and waiting, suddenly, Diane was pregnant! Miracle of miracles, she conceived right away. This was the baby that she and Tim wanted so much! Praise God!

Chemo has a bad rap, and rightfully so. As Diane tried to have good come from all things, she said, "It's amazing what clarity comes when you are stripped down to nothing." She never asked, "Why me, LORD?" In fact, she thinks of the children who experience this same horror. Diane never thought she was special — even though so many of us know she is. Her heart hurt for others, especially the children.

She was determined to be a *Super Hero*. She always had been a high achiever. She would beat all odds. She repeated again and again to herself, "I can do all things through Christ who gives me strength!" Understanding clearly that we live in a broken world, that no one is immune to suffering, Diane learned to find joy in even the worst of circumstances and to truly believe that God is working for good in ways that we cannot possibly understand.

And beat the odds she did! In 2011, Diane gave birth to a beautiful baby boy. With son Gannon snuggled in her arms, Diane savored every second of it, taking nothing for granted. It was the most awesome year!

Shortly after Gannon's first birthday, the old familiar symptoms returned. This time, Diane left her *Super Hero* t-shirt in the closet. This time, she was looking mortality right in the face! The grim reaper was parked at her door; no, he was inside her very body. Depression encompassed her as she was thrown into early onset menopause.

This time, she had a son who needed her. She had even more to live for. Following horrendous surgeries and more severe treatments, Diane was weak, sick, and tired. She was restricted from carrying anything – even her baby boy. Can you imagine a toddler with the brightest, biggest blue eyes in the world, running with his arms outstretched begging his momma to pick him up and hold him?

Diane folded; that *Super Hero shirt* was not all it was cracked up to be. She gave herself permission to be human. She was angry. She was mad at God. She really let Him have it. She begged for relief and comfort and for healing, for some resemblance of normal.

The prayer covering grew heavier and heavier.

In time, Diane began to fully trust God. She literally *prayed through the darkness*. She made up her mind that God's light would shine through **any** darkness. She would stand a little taller; she would smile a little bigger; and her light would shine a little brighter to help someone else. She talked to herself – or was it God doing the talking? – "God will take care of me! Everything else will fall in place!"

Tim's sister, Amy, had always wanted a sister and, when Tim brought Diane into their family, she finally had the sister she had wished for. She stood by Diane's side through good and tough times. At one point, Amy offered to be a surrogate should they ever need her to carry a baby for them. While Diane still had hopes of carrying another child to complete their family, Amy's gesture was one of the most generous that anyone could offer. Diane loved her even more for it.

Little did she know they would one day take Amy up on this offer. And little did Diane know how completely humbled she would be to accept such a gift.

By 2015, all hope for Diane to carry another child was gone. Three viable embryos remained, giving Diane and Tim a 50/50 chance. However, Amy was completely confident. With the support of her husband and her two sons, Amy began the grueling procedure to become a surrogate, to carry her brother and sister-in-law's child.

Initially, Amy was told that it was possible that all three embryos had a chance. Amy admits to a twinkling of apprehension as the pregnancy took hold, but she told herself that if the LORD wanted her to carry triplets for Tim and Diane, then she would carry triplets! Early on, they learned that one embryo was strong and healthy and a baby girl would bless their family. The shared joy and excitement throughout a high-risk pregnancy brought the whole family much closer together.

On July 14, 2015, Diane and Tim received the greatest gift that anyone could ever give. Their daughter Hannah was born.

Diane shares another favorite scripture:

> "So in the course of time Hannah became pregnant and gave birth to a son. She named him Samuel, saying, 'Because I asked the LORD for him.'" 1 Samuel 1:20

This was Hannah's prayer and a significant reason why Diane named her daughter Hannah Faith Michelle. Diane describes Amy as "a true woman of grace," and Amy's smile as she pushed that final push is etched on Diane's heart. Soon after, Diane held her baby girl in her arms. At that surreal moment, Diane was both Gannon and Hannah's mom.

Through the tough times, Diane has learned to trust God's plan completely. She has such purpose in her life. In addition to being Gannon and Hannah's mom, she wants to honor God by helping others who have bald heads, dark days, and cannot pick up their babies. Her favorite song is *Our God is an Awesome God* which she sings over and over every time she has a CT scan. She continues to dream big, knowing *the rest of her life is the BEST OF HER LIFE!*

The Delicate Balance

Like most young girls, Pat dreamed about who she would marry. Then, in a blink of an eye, Pat was folding clothes for a family of three young boys and her husband. In love with the man of her dreams, the man with whom she would share all of her tomorrows, Pat was ready for whatever life brought her way. She was thankful for Jim, who really understood loyalty and commitment. They had grown up together, emotionally and spiritually. He was her life.

Shortly after their marriage, Jim was drafted into the Army and eventually stationed in Fort Dix, New Jersey. Living on a private's pay, they found a 1949 Ford for $75. The car was in dire need of a paint job, so Jim painted it with a paint brush, bringing a lot of curious looks and comments from strangers. Reflecting on that years later, they felt blessed that they the ability take adventurous day trips around the state.

Jim was known not only for his poetry, but for poking fun at Pat (ALL in love!), and for several years, was asked to write a comical poem for their annual Sunday School Class Christmas party. Most of those poems poked fun at different members of the class, but one year, Jim decided to include something about Pat in one of those poems, stating *he thought she had big boobs and money and after they married, he found out she didn't have either!* Well, some newer members of the class were a bit horrified, but the others knew that was an expression of true love. The final words in one of his poems to Pat read:

Now it matters not how long God will allow

this time on earth and should it end just now,

My only prayer is that first you will go,
leaving me behind

For only one short moment, if the LORD will be kind.

'Cause I don't want you lonely or to hurt over me

and one moment without you is
all I can stand, you see.

God was important to both Pat and Jim. They tried to
stay in step – through tonsillectomies and broken
bones. The ultimate test came when their youngest
son, John, was in a motorcycle accident. This was Pat's
first real "shattered dream." There were many nights
not knowing if he would live or die, and several death-
bed vigils where Pat and Jim begged God to save their
precious son. They felt helpless. They also felt God's
presence – even when they heard the fateful words
from the doctor, "John will never walk again." Their
beautiful baby boy was paraplegic. Suddenly, Pat felt
like she was living a nightmare. Her heart broke. Her
spirit, once so lively and full of hope, plummeted into
a deep dark hole.

Jim began to pray, "Please God, help Pat and me to
help You make a blessing of this." Are you kidding?

Pat looked up at Jim like he was a total stranger! A blessing? Our son will never walk again and Jim wanted to help God make it a blessing? Shock and disbelief filled her soul. Along with that shock, Pat began to realize she had become much too dependent on her husband. When devastation comes to a child, it's difficult for parents to comfort one another.

Jim wrote this poem during the uncertain struggles with son John:

"The Delicate Balance"
by Jim Crowell
Love is the delicate balance
Which sustains a soul so dear
Just a gentle voice, a caressing hand
Or a prayer for one in fear
A slender thread between life and death
Or in moments of despair
Brings hope and courage
And life-saving strength
To one who needs our care

Mother Teresa once said, "Sometimes we don't know Jesus is all we need until He's all we have." Pat began searching scriptures. Drawn to Romans 8:28 (*"And we know that in all things God works for the good of those who*

love him, who[a] have been called according to his purpose."
Romans 8:28), she really could not see John's situation
working for good. Then the previous scripture, verse
26, caught her attention: *In the same way, the Spirit helps
us in our weakness. We do not know what we ought to pray for,
but the Spirit himself intercedes for us with groans that words
cannot express.* Pat began to really feel God's presence.
The Comforter was with her. She began to feel that
she would make it through the most tragic challenge
of her entire life. Little did she know what the future
held.

Five years later, Pat's world came crashing down! The
man of her dreams, the father of her sons, and the
husband who had loved her and taken care of her for
over three decades, died of a sudden heart attack. As
she stood before his grave, Pat did her best to pray.
She needed to be strong for her sons; they had lost
their father and their best friend. Once again, the Holy
Spirit had to groan on her behalf.

For weeks following Jim's death, Pat prayed not to
wake up each morning--it was too hard to face another
day. Her life was shattered. Her dreams were gone.
However, it was not God's plan that Pat would not
awake; each morning she awoke and she cried. She began praying the same prayer that Jim prayed when they

had sat beside John's hospital bed, "LORD, help me to help you make a blessing of this." She had to force the words through her trembling lips. Then, it began happening – The Holy Spirit began working in Pat's life like never before. She felt God's presence with her every minute, renewing her just a little bit more. Each day, she grew stronger and closer to God.

The year before Jim's death, he had begun teaching a Bible study in their home. Initially, Pat was not overjoyed about it. Even with a busy schedule, she'd have to make sure her home was readied every week. She could think of dozens of reasons not to have these people over. A year later, they were the very folks who became her primary support after Jim died.

Pat prayed for patience. She was lonely, even though at this point, she had many close friends. Her sons were still the center of her existence, and she'd even been blessed with grandchildren. Her life had purpose and she had peace. At some point, her prayers began to include the possibility of having a companion in her life, someone to help fill the lonely hours when it was quiet and calm (Pat has never done "quiet & still" well…). God sent her aging DAD to live with her! This is not at all what she had in mind! She laughingly says that we need to be very careful what we pray for. Be specific.

Three years after Jim's death, Pat met Al at church. He was handsome, a corporate pilot, and soon began to love Pat with all his heart. Pat says "there are no co-incidences in life......they are GOD-incidences, and I love the way God puts the pieces of our lives together when we let Him have all the pieces." The pieces of Al and Pat's lives were splintered and broken – his through divorce, hers through death. They married, combined families and households, and had great times together. Al became active in Pat's church and together, and they continued the pattern of having a weekly bible study and hosting many gatherings in their home. However, God's plan did not include Pat and Al growing old together. After 13 years of mar-riage, Al, a vibrant, picture-of-health handsome man, was diagnosed with a brain tumor and died one year after his diagnosis. Once again, following a year as a care-giver, Pat was alone.

When you see Pat, her shattered dreams are not evi-dent. She beams. Her smile and laughter light up the room and they are contagious. People would never know that she may have just come from helping her son John with new bandages and encouraging him to face life's increasing challenges.

Through it all, Pat beams with joy. It's not the kind of joy that comes from continuous happy circumstances. It's not joy from an easy, comfortable life. But she has learned to run to God. She prays fervently. She finds comfort in God's Word. And she surrounds herself with Godly, positive friends who love her very much.

Pat has been teased about how men seem to be drawn to her. At one time, we even labeled her as a "male magnet." On a girls' vacation in Branson several months following Al's death, she was walking around an outdoor mall. She struck up a conversation with a couple of guys talking about the shows in Branson that they liked best. One of the men asked if she would like to go to a show the next night. Pat quickly replied, "I'm here with my girlfriends! Besides, I've buried two husbands; I'd be real careful getting too close to me!"

Pat never misses an opportunity to tell others about our LORD and Savior and how, without His love and comfort, she doesn't have any idea how people make it through this life. She describes the importance of prayer and how *prayer helps keep our Spiritual closet clear of unhealthy emotions*. Thankfulness and praises are always a part of any conversation with Pat.

Four years ago, Pat met Bruce – a blind date arranged by mutual friends. Bruce had been a caretaker for his wife the last eight years of their long marriage. He knew heartache. He knew what it was like to have the world fall apart. And he knows the LORD. His first question before his blind date with Pat was, "Is she peppy?" Wow! Bruce had no idea just how peppy Pat is!

Blessings came to Pat in 3's. Three wonderful sons, and now husband #3.

Shattered dreams: Yes. Blessings? You betcha!

Life After Life

Even though my sister, Rita, was great about monitoring our Momma's care in the nursing home, we always asked her directly how she was feeling and stayed alert about any possible mistreatment. One day, I leaned down to her wheelchair level and looked her straight in the eyes and said, "Mom, do you hurt anywhere?" She was spunky and had a way of mimicking right back the action you just showed to her. So she gave me that same stare and said, "No, do YOU?"

Momma "came and went" during the last few months of her life. On one trip with my son, Wade, she didn't recognize us. She would look at one of the nurses and say, "You look a lot like my Vickie." No one could convince her that her Vickie had traveled from Dallas with her son just to visit her.

It was always thrilling when we had a few minutes of *knowing* with her. A sweet look of recognition, a smile. Hugs were priceless. When she *went away* for a few minutes, I told myself it was her quiet time with God. And in a few minutes, she would be back with me. Activity seemed to heighten our chances of a good visit with her, so I began talking with more expression; sometimes singing would do it. Dancing was my final resort, almost to the point of jumping up and down. Sometimes, she would even giggle at the person making a complete spectacle of themselves in the lobby of a rural nursing home. After one of these especially-active visits, my older sister, Jody, came to visit her 30-40 minutes after my visit. Mom was clear headed. She said, "Jo, I'm worried about Vickie. She acts really nervous." Jody laughed.

After my mother died, several months passed before another trip to Iola, KS. By then, my parents' tombstone was complete with both names and their birthdates and the date they died. The Iola Cemetery was only a one-mile walk from my sister's house, and it was a nice day for a walk. I felt it was time for a real pity party--my plan was to cry and cry and cry, to really mourn. After all, that's healthy; the therapists say so.

Seeing their names and dates on a cold, hard stone was a surreal experience. After all, they were the first people to welcome me into the world. This was the woman who carried me in her womb for nine months.

I stared at that stone. No tears. To facilitate my plan, I tried kneeling. Even on my knees, tears still didn't come. However, prayers of thanksgiving filled my soul! My arms reached to the skies and gratitude filled my heart and my mind. Thank you, LORD, for giving me these two people. They held me. There was never a day in my life that I felt unloved. I knew they loved each other - something important to a child. Divorce was a meaningless word.

Where were the tears? They come when the speed-dial on my phone lights up Mom's old phone number and I know she will never answer. When my grandchildren are playing and laughing; it would bring such joy to have her with me sharing in those good times. She loved to laugh.

And then it hit me that God promises us Eternal life with Him. That's where my mom and dad are. Would they want to return from a place of perfectness? No pain, no suffering, no tears? No way!

And the greatest comfort of all: The Bible reassures us we will see our loved ones again in Heaven!

"He answered, 'While the child was still alive, I fasted and wept. I thought, 'Who knows? The LORD may be gracious to me and let the child live.' But now that he is dead, why should I go on fasting? Can I bring him back again? I will go to him, but he will not return to me.'" 2 Samuel 12:22-23

Lesson 12: Choose Joy

He won her in a car race.

Bobbi

It all began in a restaurant in Ft. Scott, Kansas. A guy named Jim had one of the first convertibles with a retractable top. You didn't see many of those in Ft. Scott. Jim's was red and white.

Jim came into the restaurant and asked Bobbi for a date. He wanted to take her to a nice steak restaurant in town, one she had never been to. Bobbi was so excited! She took her paycheck straight to her favorite shop and bought a red skirt and a red polka-dot blouse to match the red and white convertible.

Harry, a stonemason for a local company, had also noticed the cute waitress at the local restaurant. A co-worker told Harry that she was dating Jim. Unbeknownst to Bobbi, Harry approached Jim and told him he would "race for that girl." He believed his long green Chevy Impala could beat that convertible. Winner take all…the loser would agree to walk away and never pursue Bobbi again. Bobbi and Harry's grandchildren love this story – their Grandpa won their Grandma in a car race!

A big wedding was to be followed by a honeymoon in Canada; however, Harry's dad died the very evening they were married. Instead of gazing at Niagara Falls, the honeymoon was a wake.

Five children, born 13-months apart, blessed this union. One trying day, the "blessings" were overwhelming. Each child was either screaming or crying. Harry worked out of town, and Bobbi was at her wits end. She gathered the children, grouped them in a family circle, and began crying, too. The children were so shocked that the crying subsided, and the afternoon was much more enjoyable.

In 1986, Bobbi and Harry watched as floodwaters rushed into their home. Before long, the house was covered with water which reached 25-foot depths. They lost everything - everything except a home at 1313 National Avenue.

Years before, a lady walked into Bobbi and Harry's mobile home sales center and found a 14'x52' mobile home that she told Bobbi she "had to have." She needed the mobile home to be near her son in Colorado and was willing to trade her small home on National Avenue for it. Bobbi explained to her that they sold mobile homes; they had never traded. The lady returned week after week until Bobbi told Harry that she had to at least go look at the home up for trade – after all, this mother really needed to be near her son. Soon after, in addition to a KOA Campground business, a mobile home park, and mobile home dealership, Bobbi and Harry ventured into the Ft. Scott real estate. As it turned out, following the flood in 1986, the home on National Avenue was the only thing they owned that was dry. Their three businesses and their family home were under water. The house on National Avenue in Ft. Scott, Kansas became their new address.

They knew what a storm could do.

One Saturday night, Harry's new weather radio announced another big storm was headed their direction. Just two nights prior, Harry had talked Bobbi into buying the radio. He'd mentioned it several times before and, each time, Bobbi would decline the idea. Finally, she gave in, and off they went to Radio Shack. On the way home, Harry said he would like to ride around awhile. They eventually parked by the lake to watch as the sun went down and drops of rain began to cover the lake. They'd made many trips around the lake in the 52 years of marriage. Lots of sweet memories!

Bobbi and Harry usually attended Catholic Mass on Saturday evenings. They had just drunk strawberry smoothies, Harry's favorite, and talked about the possibility of the storm. Bobbi really wanted to go to Mass, knowing that she may not want to get out in the weather the next morning. Harry wanted to stay home and rest awhile. Bobbi kissed him goodbye and headed to the church.

She returned home a little over an hour later to a quiet house. Bobbie saw Harry lying on the floor. The stillness was within him. She knew. As she lay down next to him, she ran her fingers through his beautiful, curly hair and told him how very much she loved him. She couldn't begin to count the number of kisses they shared in 52 years. She kissed him one last time, then said some prayers and one last good bye.

Next, she called 911 and then her children--"I think your dad is dead." Finally, she called their priest, Father May, to meet the ambulance at the hospital for last rites.

Bobbi still talks to Harry every day. She feels his spirit with her and thanks God for him and her wonderful children, who have grown to be wonderful, successful individuals.

Today, Bobbi is a potter. Her business card reads "My pottery is like life...never perfect and ever-changing." Visit her web site at *www.bobbikemnapottery.com.*

The lesson from Bobbi: Don't cry over what you've lost. Be happy for what you had.

She says , "It's exciting to wake up every morning to see what the day will bring"

* * *

An excerpt from the poem *The Dash,* by Linda Ellis:

I read of a man who stood to speak at the funeral of a friend. He referred to the dates on her tombstone from the beginning to the end. He noted that first came her date of her birth and spoke of the following date with tears, But he said what mattered most of all was the dash between those years. For that dash represents all the time that she spent alive on earth. And now only those who loved her Know what that little time is worth. For it matters not how much we own, the cars, the house, the cash. What matters is how we live and love and how we spend our dash.

> "Yet you, LORD, are our Father. We are the clay, you are the potter; we are all the work of your hand."
> Isaiah 64:8

Afterward

No book on prayer would be complete without the perfect prayer. In Matthew 6:9-13, our LORD gives us His example, His teaching of the way we should pray.

The "ACTS" Method
Acclaim His Holiness
Confess our Sins
Thank Him!
Supplication: Pray for needs

The LORD'S Prayer
Our Father, who art in Heaven,
hallowed be thy Name.
Thy kingdom come.
Thy will be done,
On earth as it is in Heaven.
Give us this day our daily bread.
And forgive us our trespasses,
as we forgive those
Who trespass against us.
And lead us not into temptation,
But deliver us from evil.
For thine is the kingdom,
And the power, and the glory,
for ever and ever.
Amen.

My 11-year-old grandson, Max, is one of the contributing authors of Prayer Bubbles Journal. He chose The LORD's Prayer as the focus of his narration. Don't you love the faith of a child? God does.

From Max

The LORD's Prayer helps us to pray. In my opinion, you should start every prayer with this one. If not start, end your every prayer with this prayer.

God is great and Satan stinks! None of us know what Heaven looks like, but we know it will be greater than anything we can imagine. And the thing that makes Heaven special is that we will be with God forever.

Yesterday has already been and now is gone. Tomorrow may never come. But today is a gift and that is why it's called the present. God will provide for us one day at a time, no matter if it's a good day or not.

God gives us everything so we should give at least 10% back to Him. In other words, if you had a dollar, you would give God a dime. This offering is like tax; it can help churches run smoothly and feed the poor.

It is important to ask God to forgive us because all of us sin. This has been in our blood for a long time, ever since Adam and Eve. We sin because of Satan and Satan sins because he is stupid. We need to ask for forgiveness every day because we sin every day. Temptation is all around us so we need to be careful. But with God's help, we can resist Satan. And we must try our best not to sin. But even if we fight hard, Satan is against us. But God is stronger than him and one day, He will defeat Satan! And He will deliver us from evil and when He does, everyone will huddle together and sing "Kum Ba Yah!"

At the end of the world, when everybody is dying, a light will shine and Jesus will appear and take all of the Christians to Heaven with Him. This is the prophecy of the Bible that everyone shall hope to fulfill. This day may be the end of the world, but shall be the best day for Christians because we will live with God forever and ever and ever!

You should consider adding the LORD's Prayer to your daily life and cherish it because the LORD is special and you are, too.

Max V. Rosenburg

End Notes

1 When we were at our church in Hot Springs Village one Sunday, a special service was offered for babies that have been aborted. We took cards as a commitment to pray every day for these babies. On the card was a place for a name of our choice: Spring.

2 Finer, Lawrence B., and Stanley K. Henshaw. "Abortion Incidence and Services in the United States in 2000." Guttmacher Institute. N.p., 01 Jan. 2004. Web. 02 Sept. 2016.

3 A 1986 film based on the 1960 musical comedy by Alan Menken and Howard Ashman, Little Shop of Horrors.

4 Source: Gould, Joe, Clare Trapasso, and Rich Schapiro. "Worker Dies at LI Wal-Mart after Stampede." NY Daily

5 "Discontent" first appeared in St. Nicholas (3:247) February 1876. It was reprinted in Jewett's Play Days, 1878, and again in Verses 1916. Each text is slightly different. Edited and annotated by Terry Heller, Coe College

Acknowledgements

I'm convinced that the four most powerful words in the English language are, "I need your help." It has been heartwarming to find that people are so willing to give of their precious time and talents to help me. Within minutes of sending an email asking for opinions and guidance, responses flow back into my inbox from other authors and dedicated, loyal friends. These are busy, busy people!

A feature on one of Frank Ball's blogs really spoke to me:

> My dear storytellers, don't be unduly alarmed by the fiery ordeals that come to test your writing ability, as if this were an abnormal experience – 1 Peter 4:12.

I so appreciate Frank Ball. His workshops and his blogs are extremely helpful. He has authored many books and is a great encourager to all authors who desire to glorify God.

A special thanks to my good friend, Peggy Pepper Wilkinson, who is the most creative person I've ever known. She has been my moral support throughout this important process, always there for me. And she deserves full credit for this book's tag line SPECIAL PRAYERS FOR SPECIAL PEOPLE. We bounced several back and forth and when she came back with this one, we both knew it was perfect.

Leslie Hamilton heads up the prayer ministry for Stonecroft Ministries in Hot Springs Village, Arkansas. She has prayed with me and for me. She spent many hours in the editing process for this book.

Finally, a big thank you to Tara Mibus. For years, she was one of the best proofreaders in my office. She did not hesitate when called to take a fresh look at my book.

About the Author

Vickie Henry grew up in Iola, Kansas, surrounded by loving family and friends. She has always cherished the gift of faith and the privilege of prayer.

A Wall Street Journal article called Vickie "America's Mystery Shopper" in a story about how Vickie helped pioneer mystery shopping as the owner of one of the first companies to offer this service. Her public speaking career evolved as she presented the popular keynote, "Would You Do Business with YOU?" to audiences throughout the world.

Vickie is married, has two grown children, seven grandchildren, and one great granddaughter. She lives in Dallas, Texas with a second home in Hot Springs Village, Arkansas.